100 Most Successful Women Around the World

Featuring the first fifty most successful women around the world. Amazing stories by amazing women that will inspire you to be the very best in every area of your life.

MARIA-RENEE DAVILA, MBA

DR. CAROLINE MAKAKA

Havana Book Group LLC
Havanabookgroup.com

No part of this publication may be reproduced, stored in a retrieval system, or transmitted in any form or by any means – electronic, mechanical, photocopying, recording or otherwise – without the written permission of the publisher. The right of Global Trade Chamber to be identified as the author of the work has been asserted to him in accordance with the Copyright, Designs and Patents Act 1988. Without limiting the rights under the copyrighting reserved above.

HAVANA BOOK GROUP LLC

43537 RIDGE PARK DRIVE

TEMECULA, CA. 92590

COPYRIGHT 2021 All rights reserved.

ISBN: 978-1-7353117-3-9

CHAPTER OVERVIEW

Introduction v

Chapter 1: Kimberly Anderson 3

Chapter 2: Teuta Avdyli 7

Chapter 3: Angelica Benavides 11

Chapter 4: Hala Bou Alwan 17

Chapter 5: Selyna Breeze Alicayos 21

Chapter 6: Maria Antoinette Cephas 25

Chapter 7: Seon (Zena) Chung 31

Chapter 8: Stephanie Cirami 35

Chapter 9: Angela Covany 39

Chapter 10: Maria Renee Davila 45

Chapter 11: Fayola Delica 49

Chapter 12: Virginia Earl 53

Chapter 13: Kandee G. 57

Chapter 14: Vinnette Grant 61

Chapter 15: Barbara J. Hopkinson 65

Chapter 16: Paola Isaac Baraya 71

Chapter 17: Ghazala Jabeen...75

Chapter 18: Rita Jairath 79

Chapter 19: Imambay Kamara...83

Chapter 20: Christina Konadu 87

Chapter 21: Rania Lampou...93

Chapter 22: Geralda Larkins...97

Chapter 23: Tina D. Lewis...103

Chapter 24: Mollica Maharaj...107

Chapter 25: Caroline Makaka 111

Chapter 26: Esha Mansingh..115

Chapter 27: Ingrid Mason 121

Chapter 28: Caterina Nuccia McCormick.....................................125

Chapter 29: Ann McNeill...129

Chapter 30: Riana Milne..133

Chapter 31: Marieta D. Monta..139

Chapter 32: Robbie Motter 143

Chapter 33: Syndia A. Nazario-Cardona 147

Chapter 34: Adaobi Cornelia Onyekweli......................................153

Chapter 35: Lenora Peterson-Muclin..159

Chapter 36: Miguelaille Pierre..163

Chapter 37: Angela Posillico 167

Chapter 38: Rashmi Raj 171

Chapter 39: Reenu Raj 175

Chapter 40: Shamila Ramjawan....................................179

Chapter 41: Cecilia Rokusek 185

Chapter 42: Jaya Sajnani...191

Chapter 43: Nadia Sanchez..195

Chapter 44: Janet Smith Warfield 201

Chapter 45: Mya Smith-Edmonds 207

Chapter 46: Poonam Soni 213

Chapter 47: Surika Sookram 217

Chapter 48: Dee Thompson 221

Chapter 49: Evangelia Vassilakou.................................225

Chapter 50: Baroness Angelika von Canal-Christie 229

Chapter 51: Randi D. Ward..233

Chapter 52: India White 237

Chapter 53: Dawn Airhart Witte 241

ACKNOWLEDGEMENT 243

ABOUT THE AUTHORS 245

- vi -

INTRODUCTION

"The Power of women comes from other women that inspire, empower, and motivate."

Al Otero, President Global Trade Chamber

There are two ways we grow in life. We either learn from our trials and errors or we learn from the experiences of others and their achievements. If you are, a woman in business, thinking of starting a business, involved actively in an organization or nonprofit, considering becoming involved in one, a mentor, a coach, a working mother, or student, or if you are simply looking for wisdom from women who have overcome great odds to achieve dreams this book will have a life changing effect on your life. Life balance is a big challenge for today's women. With family, career, entrepreneurship, children, home, health personal development and so much more. This book is like having personal mentors or coaches. The authors and contributors are successful women from many sectors and cultures that have achieved balance, daily routines, priorities and see challenges as opportunities. These amazing women are making a positive impact in the world in many ways. Find out how you can make an impact in your community.

This book will make a great addition to your library and will make a wonderful gift for any woman.

- viii -

KIMBERLY ANDERSON

I stand here today just a few years away from the milestone of 50. I find that I'm in a hurry up mode to get as much done before I hit that age and slow down a little and enjoy it. It's both the younger side of me in hurry mode, and the wiser side of me saying enjoy the journey. A fight of two wills per se. One of the most precious things we have is time; it is one of the most talked about "things" that eludes us. Here is a secret. There are two things in life that will take you everywhere you want to go and allow you all the time you need. Both things have the power to change you, shift you, or cripple you. They are your intuition and your mindset.

What if I told you that if you follow your intuition and change your mindset, you will change your life. And guess what, everyone has these 2 gifts; I call them superpowers. I can recall many times in my life where I didn't listen to my intuition, and it changed the course of my life. I remember a time when I had the belief and the mindset, that I deserved the horrible situations I was in. It also took my intuition and my mindset to get me out of it.

We all have stories. We all go through this thing called life, and we all are on a journey. Yes, I am an intuitive transformational coach. I have tested out my intuition to every level. I am a writer, author, speaker, and TV Show host. I have a global goddess platform and doing all that with the occasional mindset of am I good enough to do all this, am I this, or am I that. As my Unleash Your Inner Goddess platform keeps expanding to all corners of this world, I am reminded that it is about taking that first step. Do it anyway; do it scared; fall and fail forward. We are all brilliant, and you were born to stand in your brilliance, stand in your power, and speak your truth.

The greatest thing in life is to keep going. Remember, we are all on a journey, so enjoy the ride, learn the lessons, and then share your story, so you heal and help others heal out of their pain and situations. There have been many before us, and there will be many after us, but right now, this is our time, our time to shine, and our time to leave our mark on the world and leave a legacy.

It is an honor to be recognized for all the things I have done, and I am always looking out for ways to get my platform heard because that means I am helping others share their stories. We push through every day even while being in the midst of our own trials. You are a Goddess.

Website: https://www.kimberlyacoaching.com/

- 6 -

TEUTA AVDYLI

Teuta is a wife, mother of two beautiful children, a bestseller author, Motivational Public Speaker, Transformational and Parenting Coach. Her passion is to bring to the world an education reformed system, teaching parents super skills and how to leave a legacy of example. Her second book "Family Legacy of Love" will soon be published. Her approach is very simple: Educate, Inspire and Support so a family can be happy, healthy, well grounded, and strong enough to withstand years of difficult challenges.

Teuta has overcome many challenges in her life. She reached her own turning point when she realized how short life is; she was flung to the side of the road and knocked down on the ground by a big truck that ran over her legs three times. She was told by her doctor that not only was she lucky to be alive, but she may not be able to walk again. She is grateful and appreciates the gift of life of having the second chance. This time she wants to do differently; she wants to impact and inspire millions of lives and change the world with her unique gifts. She's motivated to help you turn your own story and inspire a positive change, so you can own your future.

Teuta is an all-in risk-taker, a women's advocate, and a piece of living evidence, a living testimony that overcame a terrible, near death accident. Overcoming fear and challenges and eliminating victim mindset are the breaking point to achieve something extraordinary. Working with Teuta, you will shift your perspective in life and own it, so you know that your future is forever in your hands, and you will achieve your full potential because sky is your Limit!

She is a multi-award winner: Ambassador of Peace, Beautiful Survivors Award, The Mayor's Award Certificate, Honorary Doctorate Award from Good News International University for an exemplary work in serving the international community and for an outstanding contribution to humanity, significant contribution to public life. Teuta been to different TV channels, radio programs, podcasts, newspapers, tabloids, and conferences sharing her message internationally.

CHECK OUT THE LINK BELOW TO READ ABOUT TEUTA'S STORY.

https://www.mirror.co.uk/news/real-life-stories/i-bike-heard-loud-bang-23288392?utm_source=whatsapp&utm_medium=social&utm_campaign=sharebar

She had the honor to be invited as VIP guest at Southeast Peace Summit in Albania 2019 and spoke at the closing dinner night before Presidents, Parliamentarians, and high influencers.

During lockdown time Teuta offered a few virtual meetings like a 7 weeks parenting course "Decoding Parenting, Family as school Love" and "Connection Antidote to Depression" under Universal Peace Federation (UPF). Teuta has contributed financially for clean water project in Guinea, Koba, where all donations have been used to open drinking water wells. In Orphan's Promise Project, she gives monthly financial help for the well-being of orphans and vulnerable children around the world. Teuta's service life is in her DNA; she could not picture her life without it. She manifests multifaceted leadership with compassion and humility.

ANGELICA BENAVIDES

Dr. Angélica Benavides inspires women and entrepreneurs from all over the world to leave a legacy that outlives impact and influence and most importantly never to be forgotten. She is known as Dr. B. the Ultimate Legacy Builder. Dr. B. helps entrepreneurs gain more visibility, exposure, and influence for greater impact.

Angélica Benavides (Dr. B) Ed.D. is Women's World Conference and Awards Texas Chapter Leader. Dr. B was presented with the Red Blazer of Excellence and Achievement Nomination Award with the All-Women Rock organization. She was recognized in Amazing Women of Influence. She has been featured on national television with NBC, USA Today, Fox, and Amazing Women of Influence. With all these recognitions, you think life has been easy for Dr. B. Ever since she was in elementary school, Dr. B. struggled and hated writing. She is a Latin born in Mexico with Spanish speaking parents; language was her barrier to learning. She was in monolingual English during elementary school. She felt lost and left behind. Dr. B has no idea how she graduated from high school because she hated school and writing. But she often wondered why other students learned and why she struggled in school?

This challenge in life led her to researching and understanding human development and Learning Theories. Her research and curiosity led her to complete her doctorate degrees in Leadership and Specializing in Curriculum. Life is not easy! After she defended her dissertation, the next day Dr. B. ended up in the hospital. Her intestines twisted during Zumba. She nearly died, and not even a year past when she was diagnosed with two types of cancer. Again, her life was put to the test! It was then in that very moment that she questioned herself, "How am I going to be remembered"? She wondered how I can live an ultimate life and leave a legacy that outlives me.

As she watched her life tumble in front, illness struck her, bankruptcy, divorce, and loss of identity. She sat in tears and thought deeply.

What am I leaving behind? How will I be remembered?

I wondered… If I do live, what will I do to help other women around the world?

That's when I thought… I want to inspire and leave a generational legacy so our children's children will have success stories. and they understand how we managed to get out of dark places during our lifetime by reading books we publish---not just a book, but a book that outlives us, inspires, and gives other leader entrepreneurs hope, courage, and steps to step into greatness. I now help bring out that book that leader entrepreneurs want to write, so together we motivate people who feel lost, broken, or might not have clarity of where they are headed. Joseph Epstein said that 81% of American feel they have a book in them and should write it. Now, Dr. B. wants to remind entrepreneurs to write a book that outlives them. Create an ultimate life, you desire and leave a legacy while making a profit.

Website

https://drb.groovepages.com/drbglobal/

Social Links

https://www.facebook.com/empresarioslatinxdeinfluencia/

https://www.facebook.com/groups/themastermanifestorlab/

https://www.facebook.com/groups/454521861851548/

https://www.facebook.comthemastermanifestor/?ref=bookmarks

- 16 -

HALA BOU ALWAN

Hello, I am Hala Bou Alwan, a proud mother to a wonderful son! My father is Lebanese, and my mom is Venezuelan Lebanese. I grew up in Lebanon. Childhood was not easy at all during the war, hiding in underground shelters or safe places. Despite all the horror outside our walls, it brought the whole family with uncles, aunts, grandparents, and cousins together in very tiny rooms. We had good laughs!

My childhood impacted me big time as I was exposed to many things for which a child should not be exposed.

I lived in Lebanon until 2005 and then moved to Dubai.

Being a single mom, my childhood, life responsibilities, and workload hit me at several points in my life. I went into depression, very dark years, and refused to take medicine apart from vitamins and some herbs (this does not mean I am right in my approach as what applies to me might not apply to you). It was incredibly challenging to pretend in front of others, especially my son and my teams that I am for which I fell in love. I am a member of the Lebanese Lawyers' Bar Association. I hold a master's degree ELLM in International Business Law from Boston University USA, and another LLM specialised in Artificial intelligence & Law from Universite La Sagesse, Lebanon.

I founded Hala Bou Alwan (HBA) Consultancy Firm specialising in Governance, Financial crimes, Human trafficking, Modern Slavery, Child labour, and Cyber crimes' advisory and training. Also, I co-founded H.A.D Consultants (Hopes. Ambitions & Dreams) specialising in self-empowerment events adhering to key UN Sustainability Developments Goals. I am an international speaker and trainer; I sit on multiple boards and empowering committees. I have written a book, authored many articles, interviews, research papers (published by Boston & Cambridge Universities, FORBES Middle East, Thomson Reuters, and many more). Prior to establishing my firms, I led two senior global roles at Thomson Reuters, TSME – Dubai Financial services Authority Authorised consultant, BLOM Bank France, Raja Bou Alwan Law firm & United Nations- UNDP.

If there is one thing I learned from all the challenges I faced, it is that happiness and love come from within. Once I got it right, I fell in love with who I am and with life. If you are reading this article, remember that you do not need anyone's approval to feel good about yourself. It's only you who creates your dreamlife. Release what is not serving your higher purpose and trust that life will give you exactly what you need at exactly the right time. Once you know that, start enjoying the miracles.

Website: https://www.hba-consultancy.com/

- 20 -

SELYNA BREEZE ALICAYOS

Every event in life represents a small dot, and as you go along with your journey, you can connect all those dots to form a beautiful picture.

Born and raised between farms and rice fields, I had no idea where the rivers went, what was behind the mountains, and what kind of life there was beyond the farms. I was gifted with a very curious and observant personality, and that includes having a business-oriented mind as well.

My parents deprived me from going to school. They believed it was just a waste of time. Helping them in the farm was torture for me. I was physically abused by my parents, but at the time I thought I deserved it because I refused to work in the farm. One day, I ran away from home, and the next chapter of agony began.

Although growing up without my parents was very difficult, I always found my way up and forward. I had to work at a very young age as a household helper in exchange for food. But I was lucky enough to have kind people who helped me and sent me to school.

I do believe that there is no coincidence in life. Everything is synchronized. For me success is getting to the next level. Each level is never the same, nor easy. I may have failed many times, and I thought I was going nowhere, but my spirit refused to give up. Even to this day, it refuses to give up. I do believe that we were all born rich in all aspects of life. Being rich is our birthright, and it's up to us to claim it. Always listen to that powerful feeling, those powerful questions inside us. We all have that curiosity about things around us and things that are beyond what our eyes can see. That is our power. We all have our own unique purpose, and we have to find that in order to have a successful and fulfilled life.

Looking back to where I started, it was a very painful struggle. I was called a rebel child. I jeopardized my relationship with my family because I did not live the life they were leading me to. I lost a few important people in my life because I followed my lead and let no one rule my life. But, I wouldn't change a thing even if I were given the chance to. Everything in life is a code to progress. If you're afraid to crack the code, you'll stay in the comfort zone. Dare to be YOU. There's no one out there like you! You are the only one. There's nothing to gain from settling for a version of you less than the quality of your potentials. You are a co-creator of your destiny, so don't be scared to follow what your soul calls you to do. You all have the tools within. You all have the right answers within if you know the right questions to ask.

Love yourself. Know your worth. Believe that you're powerful enough to become whoever you want to be. With a grateful heart and a good intention, you can have it all. A successful woman is a woman who has grown and learned to love herself the right way. Always choose YOU first. Only the best version of you can serve and love the best way.

MARIA ANTOINETTE CEPHAS

"BE STILL; NOW GET IN POSITION" Learning life lessons places you on the path to success! However, you have to be open to "EVERYTHING IS POSSIBLE". A life assignment surfaced in 2015. I dismissed it as it didn't align with my life. Occasionally, I would entertain the thought and be left with unanswered questions.

By March 2020 we all started to feel uneasy as our world/lives accepted, we were in a Pandemic. Like others, I made the necessary preparations to work from home. Then suddenly an inner voice said, "BE STILL, NOW; GET IN POSITION"! Normally, many thoughts are running simultaneously, and I do not decipher the difference between me and GOD. Pushing my thoughts out the way, I whispered back, "Yes, I'm ready"! Little did I know, this would turn out to be one of the most powerful lessons of my life!

What did it mean to be still? As a mover and shaker, my brain works overtime striving to solve challenges. I had no clue what being still felt like. Each day, I leaned and learned to BE STILL, which required true effort and restraint. Discovering I had "internal healing work" which needed to be prioritized, I minimized any external outlets that disrupted the process while embracing the art of meditation. I was surprised I acquired a clearer understanding of myself, the purpose of being still, my assignments, internal messages, and the definition of Self-Care (Total well-being mentally, emotionally, spiritually, and physically). Meditation allowed me to relax my mind, body, and listen to the needs of my soul. Acquiring knowledge as all these things are in alignment, transformation can begin!

This is where my true growth blossoms! Previously, unsuccessful attempts were made to meditate. This time I succeeded! Resting on my "YES", I still didn't know who, when, how, or why. In the end, I was reminded of life's most invaluable lessons. I reawakened with the eagerness to push onward and upward! Just as I was about to take my rightful position, a familiar feeling resurfaced. It was the fear of "AM I GOOD ENOUGH"! I internally heard... "Let GO". Once I released control, the next lesson was revealed. GOD meets us where we are, placing us in positions we never thought possible. GOD has equipped us with gifts to complete His work as we journey through life BE-ing who we were BORN to BE, AUTHENTICALLY. Understanding the responsibility to do healing work, as uncomfortable as I may have felt, made room for improved focus and freedom. I saw clearly why I survived tragedies and triumphs as HE led me through specific life experiences in preparation for my purpose.

Today, all questions have been answered! I was looking outside when the only thing I needed to do was "BE STILL"! I'm NOW better equipped for success and moving forward with my assignment. The book series, "How I Met my Father", is shining as brightly as the Florida sun! I'm stepping up and into my rightful position to "Start the conversation, so the healing can begin". I pray it is pleasing in his eyes! What is your assignment that you are to share with the world? "GET IN POSITION" Maria Antoinette Cephas, CPLC, CEO, CMO & Author---The Heart of MAC, LLC The MAC Coach "Making Amazing Changes" Life Coach: Personal Development

Websites:

https://www.howimetmyfather.net

https://www.yourdestinycove.com

https://themaccoach.wixsite.com/lifecoach

SEON (ZENA) CHUNG

Agent, H.E Mr. Jim Rogers, *(The 3rd most successful investor in the world after Warren Buffett and George Soros)*

Peace Ambassador, UN PKFC *(UN Peace Keeping Forces Council)*

Goodwill Ambassador, IHRPS *(International Human Rights Protection Services*

Senior Advisor, UN Habitat Korea Committee, *Seoul, South Korea*

Cofounder & Secretary-General for KABFF *(Korean-American Businessmen Friendship Forum), Seoul, South Korea*

Country Director-South Korea Committee, IETO *(Indian Economic Trade Organization)*

I am a Korean Canadian currently living in Seoul, South Korea. As an advocate of women in entrepreneurship and leadership, I am a CEO of my own company Eva Global Holdings. Eva Global Holdings is a company specializing in communication and consulting in the field of Public Diplomacy, Trade, Finance, and Investment in International Business. The term, "Eva" stands for Extra Value Added. I deliver "extra" services to my clients and business partners around the world to reach their full satisfactions. My main motivation for my own business is to donate some of the profits from my business for international charity organizations to make the societies we live in more lovable and better for the less-privileged people.

I work in many different business and economic organizations in Korea by taking important positions, such as international business advisor for WFKB (World Federation of Korean Business), and a secretary-general for KABFF (Korean-American Businessmen Friendship Forum) and for KEEEA (Korea-Emirati Entrepreneurs Exchange Association) and a committee chair for KOIMA (Korea Importers Association). I have strong political and economic connections in Korea and abroad. I work with the Indian Economic Trade Organization (IETO), a state-funded trade promotion organization under the government of India. I was appointed as the board's director of South Korea Committee and Foreign Investors Council in June 2020.

I have hold two Master's degrees, such as a M.A in Master of International Studies from Ewha Woman's University, Graduate School of International Studies (GSIS) in Seoul, South Korea, and the second Master's degree as a M.A Specialist in International Political Economy of International Development from University of Toronto, Toronto, Canada. I have vast experiences and a brilliant track record in corporate and public relations, domestic and international business affairs, healthcare management, and international bilateral and multilateral trade issues. My high credentials and great experience would add value to my existing clients and business partners in Korea and abroad. I am also a recipient of a Dr. Sarojini Naidu International Award by Dr. Sandeep Marwah, President of International Chamber of Media and Entertainment Industry (ICMEI) which gives me an opportunity to be a recipient of the most prestigious Indian award, Dr. Sarojini Naidu International Award, 2020.

Website: http://www.zenachung.com/

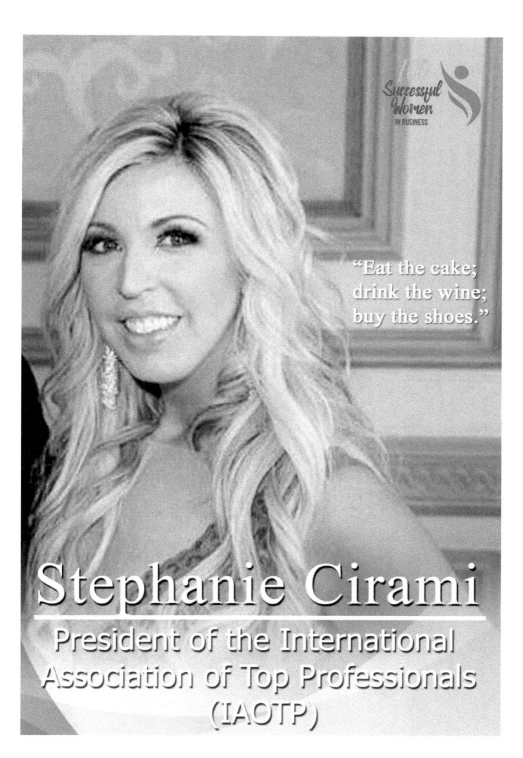

STEPHANIE CIRAMI

Growing up was a wonderful experience with my hard-working middle-class family of two amazing parents and my younger brother. My mother worked for Delta Airlines, so we traveled all over the world. My chiropractor father owned his private practice. I learned the value of a dollar as a motivated young child who appreciated everything always.

My first job was working for my aunt's International Travel Agency Jetsave, at age twelve; she taught me everything. Later I held three jobs while attending St. John's University. I worked for the Queens District Attorney's Office as head paralegal and worked for the Sex Crimes Division and Gang Violence Unit which made the show *Law and Order SVU* look like a walk in the park. I then worked for Cambridge Publishing and learned the publishing business. From Cambridge Publishing and Bristol Publishing, I realized outstanding amazing professionals needed to connect, meet each other face to face, and be recognized on a more dynamic level. This is the reason I started the International Association of Top Professionals (IAOTP.)

I possess a gift of bringing together professionals and seeing the potential of members collaborating and coming together to fulfill their business dreams, change the world for the better, and come up with amazing plans of action. Relationships are so important. The COVID pandemic made us realize how important it is to have human connection. Throughout the pandemic, our IAOTP members were still proudly able to feel connected although we could not meet in person.

I am very proud to see the amazing "collection of successful professionals" IAOTP has recognized over the past six years. I am lucky to attract professionals who have passion, share the same values, and see the importance of paying it forward to help others succeed in life.

Mistakes and failures in life are your dress rehearsal to bring you to where you need to be, so my mistakes and failures along the way were supposed to happen to bring me to where I am now.

IAOTP contributes to Stop Child Trafficking; Thorn is an important charity with which we are involved. IAOTP also donates to Smile Train, St Jude's, Make a Wish, NYLeap, Central Park Angels, Doctors without Borders, Wounded Warrior Project, Children with Autism, and NMF.

My advice to other women is to Think like a man, Act like a lady. It is ok to be an ambitious, hard working woman, who can run a company while baking a cake in heels and shuffling kids to school, karate, dance, etc. It's Nice to be Nice. What you put out to the universe returns to you. When people are nasty, it gets them nowhere. When you are kind, loving, generous, and supportive to others, life rewards you with everything you need.

Website: www.iaotp.com

- 38 -

ANGELA COVANY

According to the definition from the Oxford Languages dictionary, **Successful** is defined as

1. Accomplishing an aim or purpose
2. Having achieved popularity, profit, or distinction.

Years ago, my good friend Joan Wakeland and I had a conversation after a wonderful speaking engagement where she was speaking to the audience on the topic of "Living a Fearless Life." I had told her how I heard the Bible referenced over 360 times a verse regarding walking in faith or by faith not in fear and how I thought it was awesome to think there is a reference for every day of the year. We sat down together and were discussing what we thought limited most people from becoming successful in life. I asked her if she thought it was the fear of success or the fear of failure. I was very consciously considering both perceptions in my own life at the time. I will never forget the words that came from that question. She looked at me with the brightest smile and said, "Well, Angela, what if I fail, but what if I succeed?"

Later that day I was listening to a series of lectures on motivation, and I cannot recall who said it, but I heard them say to ask yourself, "If not me, then who?" I pondered on those perceptions the rest of the day and the value I have felt from repeating those questions has continued to propel my forward progression and has been extremely developmental to my life. If you do not pursue your passions, you will be the one watching others live out the life you wish you were living. It is important to create the life you desire. My personal mottos have always been progress not perfection and "how" is the dream killer. I started my company with the intention of being a catalyst for change to help others spread positive messages to the world through publishing. I believe each person has a unique life experience that can help others. It is an honor to be involved with amazing companies and individuals with the same intentions to recognize others with a heart to serve.

As a leader I have found that you do not need to know all the answers. You just need to trust in the unfolding and work fearlessly towards your passions with the heart to help others and success will follow inevitably. We are not here to compete. We are here to collaborate and help one another on this journey called life.

On a personal level, having the love and respect of my children, the support and guidance from my parents, and peers, and the faith from my clients are contributing factors to my success. Being a God oriented individual with good intentions, motives, and actions define success to me.

With friends, if I have contributed to their personal development, self-esteem, or motivated them I have succeeded.

With my children, if I have inspired them to follow their passions, inspired them to walk by faith or chase their dreams despite obstacles, I have succeeded. If they have seen by example, though quite imperfect and I have their continued admiration, I define that as success.

In business, if I have tried, I have already won. I have either learned or succeeded. If you do not give up, you will progress. I have heard many people say, "You don't have to be great to start but you have to start to be great." Many of us are afraid to start endeavours and it is difficult to persevere through doubt with the uncertainty of not knowing the proper steps to take which limits our potential.

To live a life filled with success and enrichment there are a few things I suggest: Surround yourself with those more educated, experienced and uplifting. We may or may not be able to change certain circumstances in our lives, but we can increase happiness by the things within our control. We ultimately are in control of our actions, our attitude or perceptions, and the company we choose to surround ourselves with. The choices we make today define what tomorrow can look like. Minimize your time with those who do not support you and/or who discourage you. Believe in your own amazing perfectly designed self and spend more time with those who value your worth and see your potential. Pay attention to your self-talk and mental chatter. Always keep it positive. When you speak it or think it, you must turn the negatives to positives.

A crucial step towards being successful is finding that one person who believes in you and getting connected with a group that you will find encouragement from in your life both personally and professionally. If you are not involved in a group that offers you such support, I encourage you to check this website below. www.globalsocietyforfemaleentrepreneurs.org

MARIA RENEE DAVILA

I was born in Bolivia where I began my modeling career when I was 12 years old. I participated at a fashion show as one of the models and won a scholarship to study modeling. That was the starting point of my modeling career. At 17, I asked my mom for help to start my company. Opening my first company was not easy at all. Because of my young age companies did not take me seriously or believe I represented models, managed an academy, or organized events. One of the biggest challenges for me was looking for sponsors; they did not take me seriously. It was so bad that I had to take my mom with me to talk on my behalf, sign contracts, and pick-up checks.

At one point I got very discouraged, but somehow, I picked myself up and did not quit. My company grew and became extremely popular. With time I expanded my services to video production and others. I had fortune 500 companies and government agencies as clients. I was a contributor in several mass media channels (TV, radio, newspaper). Unfortunately, as my company grew, my challenges also grew--delayed payments from clients, the competition underpricing services, political unrest in the country, models breaking contracts, etc. My mind and body were tired from working over 60 hours per week between the office and events on weekends. After 10 years I decided to sell my company and move to the U.S. with my husband.

Starting a new life in America was a total shock for me. I did not know the language or the culture. I went from being totally dependent on myself to starting over in a new country. I went through a terrible depression; it got so bad that I went back to Bolivia. I felt lost there not sure what to do with my life. My father told me to go back to the U.S. and study something. I took his advice and returned to the U.S. to attend the American Intercontinental University where I got a Master of Business Administration degree. Studying in another country in another language was incredibly challenging as well, but I did it!

As I built confidence, I got the opportunity to work with and for companies as an international event planner traveling overseas to do events and became a faculty member for several universities. I learned the importance of networking and building relationships to move ahead in life. My entrepreneurial spirit helped me get together with Mr. Al Otero to start the first Global Chamber of Commerce. For over 13 years we've been helping companies start, grow, and success in local/global markets. Our many services include international events, trade missions, virtual offices, digital magazine, Live Stream TV channel, webinars, seminars, and conventions, among others. Our global network gives us a tremendous reach to many markets. Our vision is to connect businesspeople worldwide. Three years ago, I created the 100 Successful Women in Business Network to connect, empower, inspire, teach, and recognize global women in business.

I am honored and humbled to have received public recognition and awards from local, national, and international organizations for my service and inspiration to many entrepreneurs and young people in many nations. My life has been the life of an international entrepreneur since the age of 17; there is no challenge too big or goal I cannot reach. The world is getting smaller and the opportunities bigger; the only limits you have are the ones you put on yourself.

FAYOLA DELICA

In looking over my life, I have had a different idea of what success would look like because I was delusional in that success is defined by what the world says it is. However, throughout my journey of life, I have come to understand that my life story helps me to define my own success. As a child of two Haitian immigrants, the American dream was to get a good education to get a good job and then to be married with children. I thought I would achieve these goals by the age of 25. Unfortunately, at the age of 39, I still have not achieved the goals of being married and having children. The world made me feel that being a single woman in my late 30s is a failed life despite all the accomplishments I have achieved in my life. Yet, after having a deep conversation with God and myself, I began to shift my perspective of success.

For someone who has had to overcome much adversity, such as sexual molestation and harassment, homelessness, and various health conditions, being alive and in the right state of mind is a form of success for me, especially during this COVID-19 pandemic. Then as we look at my accomplishments, that at the age of 24 years old, I had built my first home that was worth more than a quarter of a million dollars. As of today, I have received over 40 awards locally, nationally, and internationally. Also, I have published 9 books and a number of them have been #1 International and Domestic best-sellers. In addition, I have had over 150 speaking engagements as well as sharing the stage with nationally and internationally recognized public speakers since 2013---let alone having three degrees and working on my fourth degree. Now that is my definition of success because I would have never thought that I would be able to accomplish all this before my 40th birthday, which is in 2022. Yet, the crazy thing is that I am just warming up.

Once I understood that my definition and level of success are not based on someone else's criteria, I realized it is really based on an individual's ability to reach their own level of success. After I grasped that concept, I had been set free from the stress and expectations of others in my life. This has helped me to be more open to the flow of my creativity and ambition without any limitations. Therefore, my best advice in reaching success is by having your own definition of success. Then, my second piece of advice would be to create your own plan to achieve the level of success you seek to accomplish in your life. The last piece of advice I would give as it pertains to defining and reaching success is to never allow anyone to stop you from reaching the goals you seek to achieve. I have received much backlash over the years about doing too much. Yet, the same people who said that are the ones who have come back to me for coaching, consulting, and general advice. In reaching my level of boldness to not negotiate my level of success, I have been able to help others to do the same.

Contact information:

Dr. Fayola Delica, Your Passion and Purpose Activator

W: www.fayoladelica.com

E: info@fayoladelica.com

LinkedIn: Dr. Fayola Delica

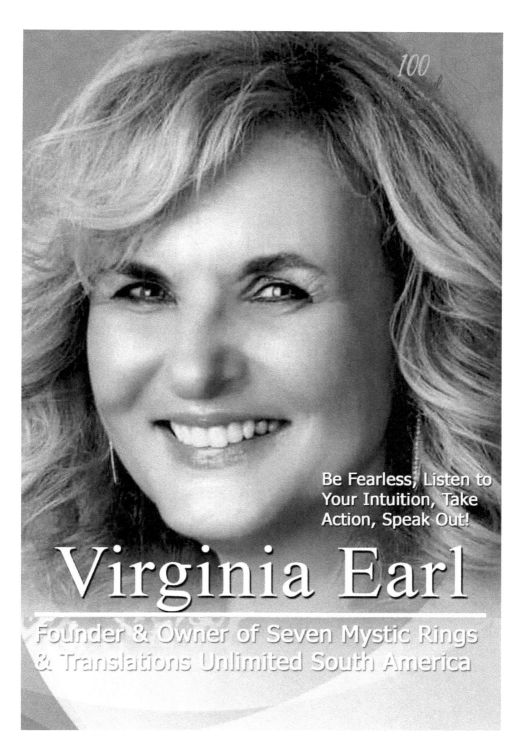

VIRGINIA EARL

Growing up in Montevideo, Uruguay, I always dreamt about writing a book, doing amazing things to help others, changing lives, and exploring faraway lands. Times were different back then. In general, people seemed to care more and had more time for each other. Families took their time to instill the meaning of respect and values while raising their children. However, in some cases parents also were too overprotective when it came to raising their children. I was one of those children. I was overprotected to the point that I was too trusting. I was so naïve that it blocked my sense of "good fear." Others protected me, but I didn't know how to protect myself.

Although it was fine because when you're a child, you're supposed to enjoy your care-free childhood; the "overprotectiveness" gave me a false sense of the real world. As I grew up, I became too trusting of everything and everyone who came into my life. Now, when I look back, I know there have been many times when I should have spoken out and when I should have made the right decisions, and I didn't. Why? Because I was afraid to take action and to speak out. My "bad fear" stifled me and blinded me!

One of the catalyst moments in my life was in 2015 when my husband passed away. I took for granted that certain things would be fine. Well, they weren't! My inner voice told me what to do and not do, but I didn't listen, and I didn't speak out. However, his death guided me into my other lifelong purpose so I could help others.

Today, through Seven Mystic Rings I help my clients identify the "why" behind their fears and roadblocks, so they can live a life of purpose and clarity. It means a lot to me when my clients say, "Virginia, you saved my life" or "You made a difference in my life."

Someone asked me once, "What is the one thing you would say to your younger self?" My answer was this: "There is a quiet little voice that doesn't use words. It's called intuition. Listen to it! It's there for a reason. Stay true to yourself and to your purpose. Remember, nobody will ever give you an award for living someone else's life, but they might admire you, respect you, and remember you for having the courage to follow your purpose, help others along the way, speak your truth, and make a difference in this world. Your courage and determination alone will be an inspiration to others."

My childhood dreams have become a reality, and yours can too! Follow your dreams and never ever stop! Leave a memorable legacy behind, not a list of regrets!

Virginia Earl lives in Murrieta, California, and is a published author and the recipient of 2021 GSFE Humanitarian Award; 2021 Women Appreciating Women (WAW) Hall of Fame Award, London, England; U.S. Presidential Call to Service Award; 2020 She Inspires Me Awards, London, England. She can be reached at (951) 551-4566 or by visiting www.sevenmysticrings.com or www.virginiaearl. com

KANDEE G

"Kandee G and I have shared the stage throughout the United States and all the way to London. Everyone has been amazed with the strategic thinking and winning approach they have gained, not only from her speeches and seminars, but her celebrated life coaching program. *Now Boarding* brings forth a great deal from that program and is guaranteed to change your life....this book will enable you to live the life others only dream about." Les Brown, the World's Leading Motivational Speaker.

Les Brown also states "Kandee G is recognized as being among the top in the industry."

Kandee G has found an incredible way to bring together her two great loves. One is her passion for making a difference, which she has done for the last twenty years with her very effective Vision Program. The other is her amazing love for horses, especially the incredible Gypsy Vanner breed. Through Equine-Assisted Learning, she uses the horses and their natural herd behaviors to teach people in a way that you cannot learn in any other form of training. It has been referred to as "playing with magic". These incredible soulful creatures have a unique way of helping you learn key life lessons that can lead to uplifting results. She has now built a beautiful training facility in Central Florida that brings her Vision Program and Equine-Assisted Training together. Corporate retreats, group and individual coaching is offered.

In an amazing way, Kandee G and her horses teach us the extraordinary power of Vision.

Check out www.kandeeg.com

www.bigsexystables.com

VINNETTE GRANT

I, Vinnette Grant, was born in Jamaica to confident accomplished parents with Cuban and African heritage. I touched down in the UK in 1960 with my mother to join my father.

Both of my parents were established tailors, and they taught me their craft, so my childhood was immersed in creativity. As the oldest of four girls, I bore the brunt of responsibility and expectations from my parents which were high. This made me strive to exceed expectations which has been both a blessing and a curse as I became a workaholic at times. My dream from childhood was to be an internationally recognized designer. I even put my athletic career and place in the Commonwealth Games on hold to pursue my love of fashion.

At seventeen I entered a relationship that I would stay in for twenty years, it gave me three wonderful children but was unhealthy and abusive. Despite the hurdles I faced I managed to study and qualify as a fashion designer. Professionally and personally, it was a challenging time for me realizing as a black woman I had to be twice as good as my white peers. My controlling spouse threatened by my talent and flourishing career was completely unsupportive. I felt like I was living a double life, the wife and mother by day, and Couture designer by night, rushing home from glamorous fashion events to become the wife and mother again, the plight of many women juggling family and career.

Through my new-found freedom I began seeking a better quality of life for my children, soon qualifying as a Flight Attendant for

British Airways. I stayed designing, producing a futuristic uniform for the company charity that raised money to support a Cape Town Nursery.

Through my inner determination I have accomplished things I am both proud and grateful for, such as my knitwear range being sold in Knightsbridge's Harvey Nichols, winning three national knitwear competitions, being shown at London fashion week twice, and being asked to create an eye-catching bridal window for one of Selfridges iconic displays, which was featured on their website for a decade, another pleasing nod. However, the things I am particularly proud of are my achievements as a stroke survivor, participating in both New York and Dubai fashion week post brain surgery and the awards I received from the Stroke Association. Since my stroke, I have been asked to speak and encourage other survivors who felt their lives were over. I have reached out to anyone who would listen in my community. I am aware that I am one of the lucky ones, but I have a lot of fight and a lot to fight for. I hope this is a source of motivation and hope for other survivors.

I don't think in terms of failure but as lessons from which one grows, learns, and blossoms. Hindsight is a wonderful thing; it is easy to put a modern, intellectual rationale on situations, choices, and decisions of the past. We are always growing; decisions made ten years ago are not the same to be made today.

I would urge people to live their truth, listen to their instincts, and never be afraid to ask for help. Have faith, don't be afraid of your light---your ability to fulfill your destiny and always be yourself.

BARBARA J. HOPKINSON

I grew up on a barrier island north of Boston, MA, USA, part of a loving supportive family of meager means, but what a blessing to live near the ocean! I studied computer science in college in New Jersey, got married, and gave birth to two healthy sons there, but I missed my ocean. After sixteen years, I fought my way back and now live on the beach on that island!

During my career in the corporate world in international technology, I worked in several industries, growing my skills from computer operator and programmer to IT Director. Then I switched to work for software companies, helping solve industry problems, including IBM for 10 years, providing large complex leading edge technology solutions to international businesses. I've been able to visit or work in 54 countries on 6 continents.

During that time, I was married for 30 years to my first husband. I became a mother, my most important accomplishment in life, raising two healthy sons, Brent and Brad. There was tragedy as well in that I lost my first baby to miscarriage and my third son Robbie was stillborn. Then my 21-year-old son Brent was killed in a motorcycle accident. My long-term marriage fell apart, my husband left me for a younger woman, and my younger son struggled in college. The impact of all that as well as an uncertain future led to an attempted suicide. Fortunately, instead, it became a turning point for me. I knew that I needed to choose to heal and to take action. I intuitively understood that helping others would help me heal. I started by founding a local chapter of The Compassionate

Friends, an international support group for bereaved families, part of the largest grief recovery organization in the world.

My next phase of life began when I met my second husband, Jim, online… He was 6'9", handsome and as nice as he was tall. His three adult children became my stepchildren; we had a blended family. Life was good… until Jim suffered a widow-maker heart attack on his way to work one morning. We had 12 wonderful years together; his children are still my family.

I was now a multiple bereaved mother and a widow. I'd lost my parents years ago and had other challenges related to loss… I fell in a gym and lost the sight in my right eye; then years later, I needed to have the eye removed and replaced with a prosthetic. I was living through many kinds of loss. Finding resilience and helping others became my purpose in life… my dream, my destiny. I started a second nonprofit, 'A Butterfly's Journey' (ABJ), and authored/co-authored several books related to my journey and what I learned. I also became an Advanced Certified Grief Recovery Method (GRM) Specialist, the only evidence-based method in the world for grief, proven over 40 years on 6 continents. I was on a mission – to help those struggling with grief, to find their hope and resilience after loss, and to encourage open discussion on grief, loss, and love.

My ABJ website http://abutterflysjourney.org contains a free Resource Center, info on GRM classes, and my passion, 'Faces of Resilience' photos. These mobile photo shoots promote raising awareness of the need for open discussion on the difficult topic of grief. Since 2015, participants are photographed expressing a phrase meaningful to them, which is written on their skin in washable marker… a visceral and cathartic experience. The professionally taken and edited photos are emailed to them, becoming a catalyst for discussion about grief with family and friends – one of the most effective ways to heal. We took these photo shoots international and released our first photo book in 2019. My dream is to expand internationally and publish themed photo books.

My advice to other and younger women is threefold: (1) Don't give up; trust YOUR gut (not others' advice); (2) Don't take things personally (most things are not about you); and (3) It's ALL about the LOVE; try to stay positive – trust that life is cyclical and will get better.

PAOLA ISAAC BARAYA

"Global trade is a conduit to PEACE & GLOBAL FRIENDSHIPS! Working together as one humanity to raise the vibration of hope, enthusiasm and creating equal opportunities through building GLOBAL BRIDGES between nations, is what I feel I came here to do!"

As the Economic Development Specialist-International Trade at the Broward County's Office of Economic and Small Business Development, Paola educates Broward businesses on exporting and developing and implements international trade policies and strategies to further the county's position as a global center within the South Florida region, the USA, and the world. Ms. Isaac assists Broward County businesses to reach global markets through creating signature seminar series, such as the **Export Readiness Seminar, 11 Steps to Exporting – A Roadmap to your Exporting Success, Doing Business with the World, Florida Export Opportunities in International Markets,** and the **Florida International Trade and Cultural Expo (FITCE)** she has been organizing for the past 5 years attracting over 2,000 dignitaries-Former Heads of States, dignitaries, and businesses from over 60 countries. She organizes international trade missions, strengthens worldwide partnerships for the county, and acts as Protocol Officer for international affairs for the Mayor and the County's Board of Commissioners. In 2020, Ms. Isaac published *"The Broward County Way – A Reference Guide to International Protocol for Broward County"*. Previously she was Executive Director for Greater Fort Lauderdale Sister Cities

International.

In 2019, Ms. Isaac's work was recognized through the **President's E Award for Export Service and the National Association of Counties (NACo) Achievement Award.** She is playing a strategic role in the opening of the **World Trade Center Fort Lauderdale.** Ms. Isaac's vision is to develop Broward County as Global Hub using a ***Triangle Strateg****y* to attract more businesses.

Her inspirational motto is stop and take a moment to reflect why it is a privilege to be here on earth and follow your inner light and guidance to learn and accomplish your true unique purpose. In conclusion, Ms. Isaac's greatest passion is to bring the world together by promoting bilateral international trade and investment which she believes will foster peace, friendship, and harmony on this planet.

GHAZALA JABEEN

Helping you present powerfully, confidently, and professionally!

I, Ghazala Jabeen, was born in Pakistan and came to the UK at six years of age. My most significant turning point at school was voicing my opinions against my family's wishes; however, my views were heard and validated. I gained confidence in speaking out for my true beliefs. I had a good upbringing from my mum and dad, which I appreciate very much to this day. My dad used to say I was his VIP = a Very Impressive Pakistani.

When I left college, I got my first job after submitting my first CV whilst still in education. I moved through my career path very well. However, the biggest challenge as a young adult was to marry against my parent's wishes. My husband, Martin, and I were married for 25 years. He was my best teacher, my best friend, and the best mentor in business I could have ever wished for. He helped me stand up in society as an equal to anyone and taught me how to best handle business decisions by detaching my emotions when doing business. He guided my career path and was my best cheerleader. Sadly, I lost him to cancer; however, he remains my strength as my Guardian Angel now.

My dream has been to become a Lady Leader to help pave the way for many women to stand proudly with their beliefs and values. I am sharing my story 'From Suppression to Expression' and now creating an impression to encourage women to speak out and be heard.

I share valuable messages during my public speaking duties, just as I did when I gave seven global announcements with my seven flags on top of the highest mountain in England and Wales. Awarded as an Ambassador for Direct Sales and Networking Marketing Industry through Business for Home and represented on their 'Hall of Fame' among great Legendary superstars in our industry, I share my successful career training for thousands of people in my teams globally.

I became a No.1 Best Selling Author for my book called *'Loved. Lived.Lost'* in less than 12 hours after the launch. As a multi-award-winning business owner with my two businesses, No.1 Marketing Machine, I help businesses with their sales and marketing for business growth. With Bollywood Burnout, I help people get fit with body transformations through my unique 80/20 weight loss program. I have appeared on many radio-talk shows, on TV and international stages, including receiving recognition and awards from excellent, inspiring platforms like LOANI, where I am proud to be a Global Voice and a Global Change Maker.

I have made many mistakes along my journey when I said the wrong things, took chances on bad business decisions, and trusted people too much without doing my full due diligence. The one sentence that helped me to correct this was 'Don't expect; always inspect'.

The biggest challenges juggling business life were having to look after our three dependent children, a sick husband, and an elderly mum-in-law, in addition to financial stress and meeting many demands left me burnt out. I have learned to rest more, plan better, and ask for support.

Website: https://www.no1marketingmachine.com/

RITA JAIRATH

Hardships for me started right from my mother's womb. My mother was a schoolteacher who fell sick with schizophrenia while she conceived me. Despite having a challenging job in Indian Air Force, my father took complete care of my mother and did whatever he could to give me a normal childhood. My challenging experience growing up in a household with mental health issues taught me a lot and shaped me into someone who is tough and compassionate. It prepared me to face the enormous hurdles of raising my autistic son and the societal judgments on my parenting. This also helped me get over the problems I was facing with my in-laws after an early marriage. Despite a traumatic childhood and married life, I believed I would be able to finish my degree. But, living in an orthodox family, everything came to a halt. Parenting an autistic child made all of it difficult, beyond comprehension. I was on the verge of failing. However, a silent spark persisted in me. I re-started and completed my education after helping my son complete his bachelor's and master's.

Along with assisting my son with his exercise, I started training, and that is where I developed a keen interest in fitness and bodybuilding. New avenues opened and my journey, from a naive bodybuilder to an internationally acclaimed bodybuilder and a fitness mentor, took a successful shape. I became one of the first women to represent India on the global bodybuilding stage. Winning the Amateur Olympia medals, a silver medal in the Arnold Classic, first place in the New York Championship, and the IFBB Pro card were among the greatest and memorable triumphs in my bodybuilding career. Now, as an IFBB PRO Athlete and the first Indian woman bodybuilding international judge from Asia, my journey goes on; it is a process. Our goals in life change as life unfolds. Building financial security, refining my entrepreneurial venture, and attempting to help my kid achieve a near-normal state despite the challenges of autism are my primary life goals. Apart from these, I want to explore my potential in other sectors, particularly in fitness coaching, classical dance, and arts.

One of my biggest dreams in bodybuilding was to obtain my IFBB pro card, which I have fulfilled. Being over 50, I realized it wouldn't be wise to compete in bodybuilding for an extended period. Since I have a family who relies on me, I wanted to compete in as many contests as possible and earn as many titles as possible. My thoughts and actions are being able to prove that age is just a number. I had a lot of victories and defeats on both personal and professional fronts. After coping with all of it and combining healthy living habits and knowledge, the biggest accomplishment and learning have come from the journey and the process, and what I have become as a person. Misfortunes and failures made me realize to respect time and opportunities. We need to grab some grit and make it happen no matter how difficult it may appear at that point in time. Down the line, when we look back at our journey, we will feel proud and appreciative. This book will set an example for women. The stories will inspire them, pique their thoughts, and encourage them to bring about a paradigm change in society and their lives.

Website: www.ritajairath.com

IMAMBAY KAMARA

Ambassador Imambay Kamara is the Founder and CEO of Disabled International Foundation Sierra-Leone, UK. She is one dedicated, inspirational, kind, and hard-working woman who has dedicated herself to help disabled people around the world and is responsible for supporting a many disabled people of all categories as well as over 5000 orphaned children as a result of the Ebola epidemic. She was born in Guinea and grew up in Sierra-Leone. She was brought up single-handedly by her disabled mother. The constant verbal abuse, ongoing discrimination, and segregation within the community because her mother was disabled was hard to take. This was the reason she decided to set up the Disabled International Foundation.

She has been recognized nationally for her work as a Disability Rights Activist/ Children Rights and Women Rights Activist earning her over 200 Awards including in America, Morocco, India, and Africa. Having experienced first-hand the challenges that disabled people face, she set out on a mission to help disabled people within Sierra Leone and other African countries and to help eliminate the negative stigma attached to them. In 2011, she was amongst other organisations that helped enforce the Policy and Advocacy on the Disability Act 2011 in Sierra Leone. in Africa. The organization directs all its proceeds to the provision of Human Rights, shelter, and the education of less privileged children and disabled people in Sierra Leone," one of the panelists said.

As an active campaigner for Leonard Cheshire Disability UK, she has helped to put policies in place for Disabled people. She has recently been a guest speaker in Geneva, Switzerland, on issues of Disability and has spoken at the House of Parliament and the Royal Institute of International Affairs at Chatham House about the Ebola Epidemic in Sierra-Leone that claimed thousands of lives. Not only is she a campaigner for Disability awareness but also to stop early child marriages. She is also a signatory to the International Female Genital Mutilation (FGM) policy implementation in the UK. Her latest project includes building a school situated in Tonkolili district, Sierra Leone, and an orphanage situated in Lungi, Sierra Leone. She is also working for Disability Empowerment Centre leading towards self-reliance of disabled people. She continues to strive to improve the lives of those less fortunate---a promise she made to her mother to tackle discrimination, stigma, and the mistreating of disabled in Sierra Leone and beyond. Her future book *Walking in My Mother's Shoes* will honour her mother Every year she hosts charity events dedicated to Education, Health & School projects in Sierra Leone as well as helping the disabled people. She is also working towards Agriculture to protect the community development.

https://m.facebook.com/DIFSIL/   www.dif-sil.org

www.disabledinternationalsierraleone.org

Email difsilceo@gmailcom

imankadie@live.com

Tel:07826893992

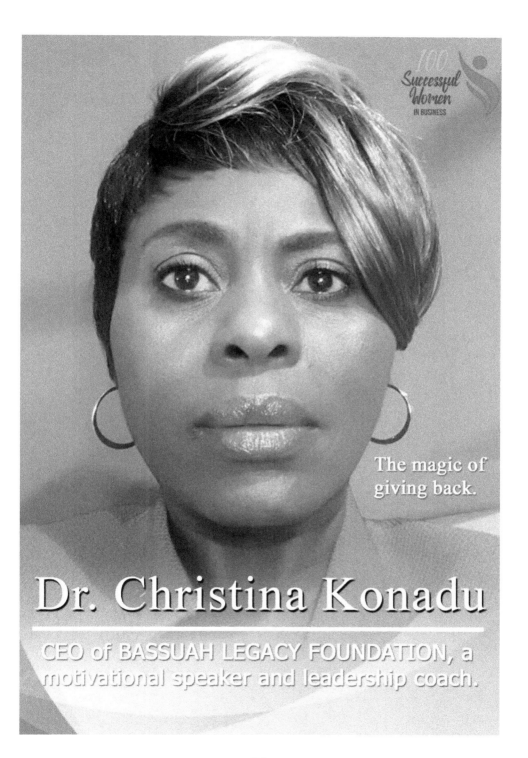

CHRISTINA KONADU

The magic of giving back.

As a young girl, my mother confessed to me that she was the happiest mother in the neighborhood after having me because each time she had no money to keep the home running, she would take me out for a casual walk and by the time she would return home, the gifts and money she would have received on my behalf from strangers and the townsfolk on just one walk with me to the town center would be enough to care for me and my siblings for up to a month. While in school as a teenager, I excelled in both academics and sports, winning competitions, receiving several awards, and fully funded scholarships. Sadly, all these were turned down by my mother who insisted I should leave these things to my male siblings and focus on house chores because as a girl I needed to take care of my siblings whenever she was away. This caused me much grief and emotional trauma growing up.

After such a challenging childhood, I promised myself to be a better mother to my future daughters. I eventually got married with my first child being a boy. I decided to try again for a girl, but after three attempts, all being boys, I decided to stop there. Soon after my last child, I became a widow after losing my husband through a terrible series of events. From then on, another challenging journey had started, lasting for about 3 decades. Through my own struggle as a single parent, successfully raising my children to become productive members of society, my dream was reaffirmed: to help and support as many single parents as possible through BASSUAH

LEGACY FOUNDATION working as a health professional in British NHS for over 20 years. Single-handedly raising my children to become prominent young men in society without family support, I established BASSUAH LEGACY FOUNDATION to support single parent families in UK, Africa, and beyond. I obtained a doctorate in Humanities and became a motivational speaker and coach to women. Through my challenges and accomplishments, I learned that all children--boys and especially suffering girls around the world--were my children, too, and that by helping their parents I would be bringing hope and a brighter future to them.

Being unable to follow my own path in the field of sports is one of my biggest failures as society and my mother dictated what a girl ought to do, contrary to the many wonderful abilities and talents one may possess as a female.

The best way to overcome difficult challenges and artificial barriers is not to argue and fight with those around you but rather through great self-dedication, focus, and commitment to your goals and ideals. The BASSUAH LEGACY FOUNDATION works together with other organisations and donors to provide resources and services including basic education, employment, and other general support to single parents in need. We encourage you to join us in this amazing cause of supporting single parent families.

To the millions of women reading this, my advice is taken from a small book called "The 8 Keys to Successful Living", by Finbarr O. Bassuah which states that "someone may be responsible for whatever you have become or are going through, but you are responsible for changing your situation, moving forward". Success depends on the conditions of your own mindset. To be successful, you must be willing to be born-again (renew your old mindset).

Only by knowing and understanding yourself can you truly become successful in your efforts in life.

- 90 -

RANIA LAMPOU

I was born in Greece in October, the beginning of a new season when the first autumn rainfalls start. I have always liked new beginnings but not without completion. My childhood is full of happy memories to which I return to get energy and inspiration. Memories are stronger than the actual events; they keep me going on my long path. I grew up with two sisters and a big group of interesting relatives and friends. Indeed, I have a big collection of experiences from my childhood. School was fun, too, but there was a lot of hard work I can't forget. In my country students study very hard in order to get admitted to universities. I am grateful I made it.

My adult life is full of hard but meaningful and fulfilling work. I am working now in primary education and as a STEM instructor at the Greek Astronomy and Space Company (Annex of Salamis). It is a blessing to teach people of almost all ages. Teaching is the center of my life. I dream of a world of enlightened teachers and happy students. Sharing knowledge and wisdom is my highest life goal. This dream has driven me through my long days and long nights of hard work. It gave me 73 international awards and recognition. This dream guided me and gave me inspiration for numerous humanitarian international projects, especially for developing countries with many challenges. Implementing African/Indian projects involves tremendous obstacles and difficulties. Survival in these countries cannot be taken for granted. All this hard work invested was worth it; the impact on the community was great. The amazing work of African students and teachers and their strong message has motivated humanitarian organizations to provide equipment for filtering water and well-drilling. The heroic efforts of Indian teachers who implement my projects involve going to underprivileged neighborhoods, giving families money and food, and teaching about nutrition.

Recently, I was inspired to write a book of astronomy that addresses very young readers. "Planetary Interviews" is the book in which I put a lot of love and fun-filled hours of work. STEM and peace education are my passions. These passions have led me to a life full of action and have given me the opportunity to serve as an ambassador in many different organizations trying to promote STEM education or peace education. There is no life without failures and especially if you do a lot of things. I had quite a few failures of my own. I embrace and respect all of them, and I let them serve me.

Keep up the good work. Luck likes fearless people. Find your passion and follow it. Listen to your inner voice rather than the advice of others. Embrace your uniqueness; let it shine for everybody. Don't let anybody talk you into believing that you are not good enough. Follow your heart; success will follow. Don't forget to get valuable teaching from failures. In my life I learned that success and failure are sides of the same coin. They are both equally significant in our evolution.

Website: https://www.facebook.com/rania.lampou.16

Geralda Larkins
Visionary Strategist, Author, Pastor, and Leadership Coach

GERALDA LARKINS

Running a business is not easy, and sometimes it can be easy to succumb to burnout and fatigue when there is a lack of alignment. That is where Visionary Strategist, Author, Pastor, and Leadership Coach Geralda Larkins comes in – bringing with her a passion to inspire people from all walks of life to discover their personal power. As part of her role as Executive Director and Senior Pastor of Impart Kingdom Ministries (IKM), Geralda helps individuals plan and pursue their purpose, and build an extraordinary life and legacy.

An award-winning motivational speaker and trainer, Geralda teaches leaders how to operate in the spirit of excellence while strategically aligning people, processes, and programs for peak profitability. She founded Impart Kingdom Ministries as a faith-based organization that provides personal and professional development services to small and medium-sized organizations and their people. Services include strategic planning, business consulting, leadership development, networking events, and more. The ideals of faith can permeate many different areas of personal and professional lives in ways that drive success forward. Geralda teaches kingdom essentials for success in life, in ministry, and in the marketplace.

Within the last five years alone, IKM has launched 25 published authors and 10 certified vision strategists. The firm has also facilitated 45 business launches and 34 business expansions across 10 states. Building this level of consistent success comes down to one major advantage that Geralda has over her competitors – vision. With a signature coaching program called Vision Essentials, Geralda and her team of Certified Vision Strategists help clients map out a clear strategy to effectively move their ministry, business, or initiative from dream to reality. In the process of transforming businesses and ministries, the clients themselves become more confident, dynamic, and servant-hearted leaders.

The programs delivered by IKM and Geralda showcase deeply personal stories of growth and transformation. Geralda believes if there is ever going to be personal or professional growth, there often comes the challenge of facing fears, leveraging failures, forgetting the past, and moving forward with a clear vision of success. Geralda teaches her clients to focus on that vision, understanding the "why" behind their transformation because when the 'why' is known, the 'what' has more impact. Vision reflects the 'why', and Geralda helps her clients see it, believe it, and work hard to achieve it.

In her book, *Train Transform Transition – A Strategic Approach to the Life You Deserve*, Geralda shares her own personal transformational journey. She asserts that often times her biggest obstacle was herself. Before understanding the power of vision, she was blinded to her purpose and made decisions from a dark place, a dim perspective, and distorted position. By building on a foundation of faith, Geralda began pursuing a vision for her life and legacy which continues today through Impart Kingdom Ministries, her 20+ years of career government service, her family, and community involvement.

In everything that both Geralda and Impart Kingdom Ministries do, there is a culture of servitude. She strives to be a servant-leader, treating everyone with dignity and respect. It is this culture of servitude she also strives to instill in clients. Building a vision means often putting it into others' hands---an easier task when trust, dignity, respect, and servanthood exist.

The best leaders gain an appreciation of the diversity of the talents, skills, and gifts one brings to the table, putting them to full use and linking them to the bottom line. Impart Kingdom Ministries and Geralda understand this better than most, inspiring personal and professional transformation in business owners and leaders everywhere and aligning purpose, vision, and belief to ensure true growth and success.

Website: http://www.GeraldaLarkins.com/

- 100 -

TINA D. LEWIS

I was exposed to drugs, alcohol, and violence at a very young age, but I LOVED my childhood. Even though I went to 6 different schools from kindergarten to the 12th grade, it didn't affect how I thrived, not educationally anyway. At each school, I became a stellar student, achieving straight A's and becoming very popular. I remember winning my 5th-grade spelling bee! FIRST PLACE! The experience was exhilarating, and I was hooked! Winning became my aphrodisiac!

Being a teenager was HARD! My mom was in a near fatal car accident, and it drastically changed our lives forever. We moved to the projects, was on welfare, and even lacked necessities at times. This taught me a valuable lesson: You are not in control of WHAT happens, but you are in control of HOW you allow it to affect your life! In the midst of drugs, gangs, and violence, I refused to become a victim of circumstance or fall prey to my environment, so success was the only option. I worked hard. I mean really, REALLY hard.

I believe that's why my adult life has been the most rewarding! I graduated from the University of Southern California Keck School of Medicine and am a Physician Assistant by trade. I received a full academic scholarship! I remember while being a single mom (had my daughter when I was 19 years old), I worked 2-3 jobs at times saying, "this too shall pass" and guess what, it did! Matter of fact, it always does, and it will for you, too! I haven't worked a job or for anyone besides myself in over 20 years! I've come to the conclusion that I'm chronically unemployable, allergic to supervision and time freedom is paramount.

Today I am an extremely successful businesswoman, serial entrepreneur, and philanthropist. I earn multiple 6 figures in 3 different industries: Medical, Business Coaching, and Network Marketing as a Top Recruiter and Income Earner. I've traveled to the Dominican Republic, Mexico, Thailand, Greece, and the British Virgin Islands.

I've been to the pristine Necker Island owned by Billionaire Richard Branson whom I've had the honor of meeting personally. I've shared stages with Donald Trump, Les Brown, Tony Robbins and John C. Maxwell just to name a few. I'm also a six-time International Best-Selling Author, Professional Speaker and founder of Royalty Coaching, a Premier Business Strategy and Marketing Firm. As the #1 BottomLine Strategist, I help entrepreneurs and business owners work less, earn more money, generate multiple streams of income, and create time freedom to do things they love and enjoy! Currently, I volunteer my time, energy and resources to my community and believe it's our moral and social obligation to serve those who need it most. The stories in this book are REAL stories by REAL women who overcame and conquered. You will, too! NO MATTER what you are going through, how hard it gets or how bleak the future appears, in the end, YOU WIN P E R I O D! I've helped 100's of women. You're NEXT!

Schedule a FREE call with me today @ ChatwithTinaD.com. Follow me on Social Media: FB, IG, Twitter, & LinkedIn @ TinaDLewis or because for me business is personal, simply call 310.496.5875.

MOLLICA MAHARAJ

Mollica Maharaj is a strong woman and not afraid to share her opinions and speak her truth. She is kind, generous, compassionate, honest, willing to be vulnerable, and authentic. She is true to herself. She questions social normative roles placed on women and more especially, women of colour. She reserves the word 'Yes' for when she really means it. She is lively and bubbly with high spirits and a great sense of humour, and fun to be around.

She is the CEO of Rahman and Rahman Incorporated, an admitted attorney in Gauteng, South Africa. She has an MBA degree and other qualifications. As an established lawyer, Mollica spends much time on academia and established an in-house paralegal training programme, whereby she trains and imparts practical legal knowledge to aspiring paralegals. This training equips disadvantaged individuals to enter the legal workplace with practical legal training and acquiring permanent employment.

Outside the courtroom, Mollica spends time advocating gender equality and women's rights and developing and coaching teens and belongs to the Teenage Empowerment Forum. She coaches individuals on their personal, academic, and professional life. She is a blogger for the Institute for African Women in Law.

She has won numerous awards including but not limited to Top Performing Business Manager, Top Performing Women Leadership Awards, and Woman of Award 2020 and has been featured on radio and television on many topical and legal issues. Passionate about the law since high school, she knew this was the profession for her and joined it to help people.

Mollica comes from a humble, very conservative Indian family in South Africa. She is the wife to the CEO of Endorphin Global, Akash Maharaj with 2 daughters, Shivalay and Shivarthi, and her dachshund Rani, a key part to complete her family. Mollica coaches her 14-year-old daughter, a social media influencer and motivational speaker. Dealing with loss of her role model mother has been one of Mollica's biggest challenges.

She lives by the motto, a positive attitude attracts a positive life and exudes an attractive charisma. Her personal slogan is "your today does not define your tomorrow".

Website: www.rr-inc.co.za

- 110 -

CAROLINE MAKAKA

Professor Caroline Makaka is a woman of many talents and an expert in many industries---

A lady with a vision and a mission to shape the future of the world. She is the Founder/President /CEO of LOANI - Ladies of All Nations International, Creator of We Are the Change World Movement. Her areas of expertise encompass a wide range of skills such as Philanthropy, Global Leadership, Non-profit Leadership, Charities, International Project Management, Human Resources, Leadership and Individual Counselling, Equality & Diversity, Youth Empowerment and Recognition Awards.

She was born in a family of six girls and one boy in Africa. They lived a pretty much modest livelihood. Her dad provided all the needed basic stuff; they attended fairly good schools. However, tragedy struck when she lost both of her parents within a few years of each other. As a young girl, her life immediately changed. She faced some challenges that shaped her into the woman she is today. As an adult she made it a point to help others. Her mind shifted from "I can do this" to "l must do this." We don't grow when things are easy. We grow when we face challenges. So first, she studied and obtained 2 degrees, a B.S. in Human Resources and Management, a Master's degree in International and Global studies, and a Doctorate degree in Global Leadership and is now a professor of Global Leadership and an Honorary Professor for Global Leadership of Humanitarian. She is a lady with huge dreams and a vision and a mission to shape the future of the world and to help and support the underprivileged.

Her dream is to eradicate poverty on earth. Caroline does not look at awards as success. Her accomplishments are determined by the success on the ground, how much, how far, and how many she has helped. Her organisation LOANI in more than 165 countries has helped widows and orphans.

Caroline states, "I have learned to Lead by Example, someone who leads, inspires, and motivates others seeking to know the better version of herself. This helps me to build my positive growth and mindset while helping others to strive and reach greater heights. I do not give up easily. In my vocabulary failure does not exist, only setbacks. Whenever I do not get what I want, I dust myself off and try again. We have had issues accumulating funds and project sponsorship, especially during this pandemic, but we never stop. My mission statement is I Aim to achieve. In everything that I do, I aim to achieve. I created Ladies of All Nations International (LOANI), a global platform creating opportunities for business collaboration, spreading knowledge, and inciting ideas and thoughts to create a beautiful new world, especially for women who need to strengthen themselves. We have charity events, educational seminars, and workshops to empower the impoverished, specifically in third world countries.

CHANGE STARTS WITH US! Becoming successful is sharing a vision. Remember to engage both people's hearts and minds. As successful leaders we are always learning; change is constant. If we are persistent enough, success will definitely come our way.

Email: Loaniworldleaders@gmail.com

Website: www.loaniinternational.com

LinkedIn: Dr Caroline Makaka

Instagram: @Loaniglobal

- 114 -

ESHA MANSINGH

I am Esha Mansingh (35) – a young business leader, women empowerment change agent, a media personality, and a multi-award winner with a passion for driving impact and change in business and communities. Above all I am a mum to two beautiful kids, a wife, and a daughter.

My story in the listed corporate world spans over 12 years and has culminated into my current role at JSE-listed Imperial Logistics where I serve as the first and only woman and youngest member of its executive committee. This role has equipped me to drive Imperial's purpose, which is closely aligned with my personal ambitions to empower others and uplift communities. I am chairman of Imperial's first global women's forum, and I steer the group's CSI initiatives across Africa and Europe, aimed at developing communities and empowering women, primary healthcare, and education. I serve as a non-executive director of the Imperial and Motus Community Trust, Unjani Clinics, International Youth Society South Africa, and the vice chairman of Ladies of All Nations International – South Africa chapter.

I spent the formative years of my life in Chatsworth, South Africa, and matriculated at Pinetown Girls High, where I also served as the Deputy Head Girl and Chairperson of the school's Learners Representative Council. Being the youngest of 4 children, I was fortunate to have grown up in a household where my parents sacrificed much to give me opportunities to progress in life.

Being an ambitious young woman, I always wanted to make an impact and inspire others to make an impact, too. I believe that there is so much need in this world, and no matter how big or small, we can all make a difference and contribute in some shape or form..

While my life may seem glamourous, my journey has been challenging. Having served as a young female in the male-dominated mining and logistics industries, I have had to work extra hard and prove myself over, just to be recognised. I have learnt that you create your own voice and should take any opportunity that may arise, whether or not you believe you are able to excel at it. There have been many times when I failed – but failure is part of the journey. The trick is to not let failure overcome you but to take those lessons and use them to progress further. Always keep your eye on the bigger picture.

I live by the motto 'always dress the part'. Being able to motivate and convince myself of the value I am adding every day despite my age, gender or background has empowered me to succeed. Being surrounded by other successful leaders that create opportunities for others is invaluable. I have also learnt that changing the narrative cannot be achieved alone – we need the support of our colleagues and business leaders.

Being successful and juggling many roles at the same time is not easy. We should always take time for ourselves – the world needs us to be healthy and happy to make a difference. To my fellow women: Don't be apologetic about being a woman; be authentically you! It is easy to feel the pressure to be something other than yourself, but don't underestimate the value you can add. It is pleasantly surprising how traditional feminine traits, such as empathy, a motherly instinct, and nurturing can set you apart and make you a great leader. And remember – 'always dress the part'!

Website: www.imperiallogistics.com

- 118 -

INGRID MASON

I was raised by a single mother who migrated from Haiti at an early age. She worked hard to make sure that my sister and I had the life she wanted. She spent countless hours making ends meet. She didn't want us to see her struggle, so she kept us busy by putting us in different outreach and magnet programs. Because of her example, I became ambitious and resilient.

I met my soulmate, the man of my dreams. He played a big role in defining who I am right now as an adult; he is my biggest supporter. We got married and had two beautiful, amazing daughters. As a family, we set the bar high. We want our daughters not to settle for anything less. We do it by being the best example for them, making sure that they have something to look back on, so they can be able to continue to the business where they can flourish. One of my recent accomplishments includes becoming a Certified Wedding Planner. I also received my AA in Mass Communication and Journalism, and Bachelor's in Management Information System.

I learned nothing is going to be given to you or handed to you. If you want something done, you must make sure your heart and soul is 1000% committed. My husband always reminds me my word is power. The more you speak to what you want into existence the more it comes to you. I have failed a lot before, and I'm sure I'll be failing a lot in the future. There are failures where I know I did my best but still failed, and there are those where I know I just did bad. Whatever failure, I make sure I use those experiences to learn, dissect, and reteach myself. I don't believe experience is the best teacher; it's incomplete. "Processed" experience is the best teacher. Challenges are understatements---little obstacles along the way. What I had were wild animals ready to snack me anytime. Life is never an easy road. We all choose a path; it takes a strong person to stay on track. Like my mom, I have also had times where we struggled financially. What I'll teach my daughters is nobody is immune to all sorts of challenges in life; nobody can ever protect them from it, not even me. I live to make kids and even their families reach their dreams---for them to understand their potentials and be the best version of themselves. We opened a school for kids that need attention. Our school uses a holistic approach and is family oriented. We impact the community by reaching out to students who need love not only at home but also in school.

Women, you will face different types of people. Some will support you and be with you through thick and thin. There will be those who will try to break you, want to see you fail, and contribute to your failure. But no matter what they do, you choose who you are. Positive words are powerful, but negative words can be destructive. Don't let words get a hold of who you are and where you want to go. There is no limit to where you can go; there is no limit to who you can be. No walls ever exist to block you from moving forward. Your biggest enemy is you. Focus on yourself.

Becoming successful depends on your ability to be you; define what success means to you. Have a map to follow. Have the right motivation. Be positive. Be the light to others. It's not about credentials. Be vigilant, be strong, and take the lead.

Website: www.upgradeeventsbyingrid.com

Ms. Caterina Nuccia McCormick

Chairman for the Thomas W. McCormick Scholarship Fund and Chairman Emeritus for Greater Fort Lauderdale Sister Cities International.

CATERINA NUCCIA MCCORMICK

Ms. Caterina Nuccia McCormick is the Chairman for the Thomas W. McCormick Scholarship Fund and Chairman Emeritus for Greater Fort Lauderdale Sister Cities International.

She was born in Sardegna, Italy, Ms McCormick grew up in Rome since the age of two and moved to the United States as an exchange student at the age of 21. She married at age 25 to Thomas W. McCormick, a recognized Lieutenant and Captain in the U.S. Army.

Ms. McCormick lived in many countries, including France, Germany, and Saudi Arabia. She was appointed by Mayor Cox in 1986 as President of Greater Fort Lauderdale Sister Cities International where she created 17 sister-city relationships around the world for the City of Fort Lauderdale and organized and hosted the Annual Sister City Conference in 2007. She then became Chairman Emeritus of GFL Sister Cities International for life and founded the Thomas W. McCormick Scholarship Fund in honor and memory of her loving husband where she sent over 200 students to sister cities, including Rimini, Venice & Rome, Italy; Belo Horizonte, Brazil; Duisburg, Germany; and Quepos, Costa Rica.

Ms McCormick's dream is to provide local students the opportunity to study and broaden their horizon in sister cities around the world and to expand the cultural, education, business, and diversity for the City of Fort Lauderdale and Broward County to the world.

In 2012, Ms McCormick was recipient of the Distinguished Citizen of the Year Award presented by Mayor Jack Seiler on behalf of the City of Fort Lauderdale. In 2017, she received the highest recognition from the President of the Republic of Italy for her dedicated commitment to connect the City of Fort Lauderdale to Italy and to global cities as envisioned by Sister Cities' creator President Eishenhower in 1956 to promote peace around the world.

Ms McCormick learned from her accomplishments the importance of education and business exchange programs to expose the youth to the cultures of the world. Her impact in the community has been to empower the youth through educational exchanges. Her advice to aspiring women is that you can accomplish any dreams if you open yourself to other countries and other cultures which inspire peace.

Website:

https://www.twmccormick.org/

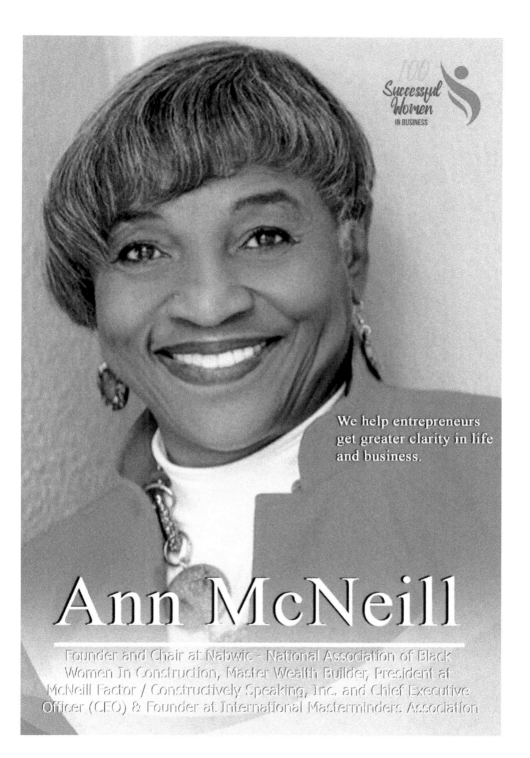

ANN MCNEILL

I, Ann McNeill, was born in the 50s in South Florida. My mother was a maid, and my father was a sharecropper, gardener, day laborer, and entrepreneur. Studying the word of God was a big part of my childhood because my mother was a holiness minister, but I did not know how to apply what I studied to my life. Because my father was a businessman, I was exposed to the world of business but didn't know how to apply that to my life either. I grew up exposed to these two paradigms – faith and entrepreneurship. This was the groundwork in the making of the woman that I am - a faith walking, talking entrepreneur.

The career path I travelled led me to being the first African American female licensed general contractor in the State of Florida to do business on the level that I do, working on most of the iconic projects in South Florida, such as the American Airlines Arena, the Marlins Ball Park, and the Philip and Patricia Frost Museum of Science. Being a black female in the white and male dominated construction industry has been a challenge, but through MCO construction, we have been able to thrive and provide sustainable employment for many in our communities, which along with the National Association of Black Women in Construction of which I am the founder and chairwoman helps me to fulfill my dream of adding value to the lives of others in the construction industry on a national and international level.

My journey has afforded me several life lessons, but one of the greatest lessons that I have learned is not to limit what I can accomplish. Of course, learning this came from the failures I made along the way. Earlier on, in my career I focused too much on money. I learned the hard way that my family and health are more important than money. I ended up losing both in my pursuit of money. My pursuit should have been of a better quality of life. I am thankful that God gave me another chance. This taught me to refocus, reset and get it right.

As the master builder I want to impact my community by helping people build better, stronger lives and businesses. I encourage people to build their self-confidence and study self-reliance. I advise that you read Napoleon Hill's *Think and Grow Rich*. It changed my life. Set goals in every area of your life for personal development. Invest $20 a month in a product that you use. Connect with your spirit through journaling. I guarantee that if you follow these tips, you will have a better quality of life.

Success happens when you have a larger dream of what is possible, know exactly how much money you want and what you will do in return for it, and know the date by which you want to accomplish this. These are some of the principals that govern my life and the application of them work if you work them.

Website:

www.annmcneill.com

www.mcoconstruction.com

RIANA MILNE

CEO of Lessons in Life & Love Coaching LLC & Therapy by the Sea LLC

It's Time to Create the Life You Desire & to Have the Love You Deserve!

I was raised in Huntingdon Valley, PA---the 4th of 5 kids to Col. Jack H. Milne Sr. and Beverly Milne-Ryan. I graduated from Penn State with a BA in Broadcasting and studied "The Masters" in Business, Psychology, and Spirituality since I was 15.

I developed "The Mindset for Success" System at age 25 which was instrumental for my Models & Talent to reach their dreams. Within 6 months of opening my Talent School, I won "Educational Excellence Award" and in one year, "International Model & Talent School of the Year."

I went back for my master's at age 37 and graduated Summa Cum Laude from Rowan University in Applied Clinical and Counseling Psychology.

In 2000 I opened my practice, *Therapy by the Sea LLC* in Atlantic County, NJ. I also worked as a SAC Counselor in schools for grades K-through college, in a Hospital Mental Health Adolescent ward, in a Teen Drug & Alcohol Facility, and with women from the prison system.

I was also an Advice Columnist for 35 newspapers, created a Business Networking Group, and was a Stockton University Professor for their Addictions' program. In 1997 I became one of the busiest Inter-Faith Ministers in Southern NJ.

After working with many people of various ages who experienced trauma, I did deep research to discover the solutions to help victims of Unhealed, Unconscious Childhood & Love Trauma. In 2012 I developed "The Childhood Trauma Checklist™" Assessment tool.

This research led to my #1 Bestselling book, LOVE Beyond Your Dreams - *Break Free of Toxic Relationships to Have the Love You Deserve:* and LIVE Beyond Your Dreams – *from Fear & Doubt to Personal Power, Purpose, and Success*. I also created two 150-page Coaching Workbooks for my Courses, *Dating to Mating for Singles, and Relationship Rescue for Couples.*

I went on to become a Certified Clinical Trauma Professional, and Mindset Coach and in 2017 decided to work globally as a Life, Love Trauma Recovery & Mindset Coach. I developed an App, TV, Radio Show, and podcast, all called - Lessons in Life & Love™; and have over 250 educational videos on my YouTube channel. I've been interviewed on over 750 podcasts and summits in 3 years, thus giving me strong SEO for marketing. In 2020 I won *The Delray Beach Award for Best Psychotherapist & Life Coach,* and in 2021 was honored to win one of The International *"Top 100 Successful Women in Business"* Awards. I have had a blessed career!

I raised two daughters, Alexi Panos (age 37; who appeared in Forbes & Inc Magazines as one of the Top 11 Women Entrepreneurs Changing the World. She has put 21 water wells in Africa since the age of 20); and my daughter Stephana Ferrell (age-38) is winner of "The Top 50 Photographers in the USA". I also have 6 adorable grandchildren.

My website https://RianaMilne.com offers my Free eBook, book Chapter downloads, and Free Love Tests. Links are found at https://

flow.page/rianamilne/. I wish you all the best in your career! Be sure to use expert Marketing and SEO tools to grow your business online and become Licensed and Certified in your field.

- 136 -

MARIETA D. MONTA

My name is Marieta D. Monta or Maya / Mayeth. I was born on May 04, 1976. I came from the small village of Dipag 1, Manuel Guiangga Tugbok, Davao City Philippines--one of eleven children from the same parents. Around the age of 8, I was sexually abused by my closest family. I left the village at the age of 13 to find work and a better life in the city to finish my studies. I attended college in the Philippines in 1995 undergraduate. Because of poverty I left the Philippines in 1997 when I was 21 years old for the Middle East to find a better job to support my siblings. I then moved to United Kingdom in 1999 as a private nanny and housekeeper. Sadly, I was treated unfairly and locked in the room overnight with no food to eat.

I was married to a Filipino/British citizen, but the day after our wedding my husband died of liver cancer in 2006. After his death, I was kidnapped by his relatives for the property conflict. A series of tragic events struck my life. I suffered post-natal-depression and was betrayed, used, and abused by my new partner. I was suicidal several times in life from childhood experiences to adulthood. Whilst processing my agony, I met many unexpected people who gave me words of wisdom and encouragement. In 2016 I realised I had a mission to do. I turned the pain into power. I set an organisation in my country---Maya's organisation Philippines, Inc. (MOP,Inc.) to raise awareness on sexually abused children and to help rape victims with my own expense.

My goal is to build a rehabilitation centre for children suffering from sexual abuse in the Philippines. My story as a victim of rape and now a survivor caught the attention of some people in the press in London. I was also invited to speak at many international women's organisations about my journey to encourage others and to give back to the society.

In recognition of my works and effort, I received 7 International awards. I was awarded the 100 Most Inspirational Women in the World 2019, Beautiful Survivor Award from Ladies of All Nations International and appointed as a LOANI Chairperson to the Philippines 2019 with a mission of distributing recognition awards to survivors in the Philippines. I received a recognition award from international organisation Sierra Lion Disabled Foundation and a prestigious recognition award from Global Trade of Chamber (GTC) in Florida USA. I am currently working in the United Kingdom as a private nanny to provide financially to the organisation. I also built my own MOP office in the village of Manuel Guianga with my own source of income to continue moving forward for its progress.

During this pandemic and no schools open, many children were victims of sexual abuse, especially those victims in the suburbs who live in the same roof of their perpetrator. Some children committed suicide because there was no place to go. We are offering our support to the community. We are also distributing hygiene kits to the 300 children in 3 villages. I fully dedicate my life to this mission to help and protect those who are still in the dark and suffer in silence. I would like to inspire men and women and other victims/survivors to come forward---speak up and do not be afraid to tell their stories. Always take the challenge and never give up no matter what happens and how long it takes; you will get there in the right direction. God plan's is always best.

Website: www.mopinc.org

ROBBIE MOTTER

My childhood was spent in many foster homes. I lived only short times with my mother and never knew my father. One thing I always knew is that my future was totally up to me, so I set a path to success and it took hard work, but I achieved it and more.

At age 14, I left the last foster home and got on a Greyhound bus, went to San Francisco, interviewed for an office position, and got the job. They had no idea how old I was as I looked older. I found a boarding house that let me rent a room and this was the start of my long business career. Each step moved me into higher positions, and over the years I held top management positions with large staffs. In the early 70's, I asked this woman to teach me something, and she looked at me and said, "I will not teach you or any woman." That blew me away. I could not believe what she was saying. That was the day I vowed that I would spend the rest of my life helping women and always sharing what I learn with others. I stayed committed because that is exactly what I have been doing over these decades.

I have been able to interact with thousands of women to help them step out of their comfort zones and soar higher. I love hearing about their successes and to know that perhaps I had some small part in helping them to step out of their comfort zones.

My accomplishments are my three beautiful children that I raised as a single parent and seeing the women that I have mentored and connected find opportunities to step out and step up to their greatness also touches my heart.

My favorite saying is "It's All About Showing Up and the Power is in the Asking" and this year I published a US #1 and International best-selling book on Amazon with that title and gave 46 of my GSFE members the opportunity to be in the book at no cost to them as well as our publisher Angela Covany of Havana Book Group, LLC, who was able to start her publishing company with this book.

My life had many challenges; to me a challenge makes one think out of the box and look for another way to solve the issue. From these challenges I became a stronger person, and I was able to share with others steps to help them overcome their challenges as well. In 2017, I formed a 501 c3 nonprofit Global Society for Female Entrepreneurs whose mission is to empower, inspire, educate, mentor, and connect women, so they become successful entrepreneurs. Our meetings are live and on Zoom, so because of that our members are not only Global but local as well. Check out our website www.globalsocietyforfemaleentrepreneurs.org

I have been honored many times for the work that I do with women, but the greatest honor is to see them live their dream and not let anything or anyone stop them. So, live your dream, step out of your comfort zone, know you are in charge of your destiny, and that you can accomplish anything. Keep SHOWING UP and ASKING as those are two powerful words that will help you soar higher to reach your dreams.

SYNDIA A. NAZARIO-CARDONA

Syndia is a native Puerto Rican from Rincón. She moved to the United States over 30 years ago in search of growth opportunities. Syndia has a bachelor's degree in psychology and a master's degree in Human Services and Administration. She currently resides in Washington, DC, leading the Ana G. Méndez University's (AGMU) government affairs and community relations efforts of the President's office as associate vice-president. Since she moved to the U.S., Nazario-Cardona has stood out for her active commitment to the community, for her work in leadership through education, and for her contribution to the development of bilingual education.

Furthermore, she has excelled because of her role in the insertion of graduates in the labor society as a fundamental part of this country's progress, where the Hispanic community with more than 50 million people has become the majority-minority. "I am passionate about my community; the student's stories inspire me as they overcome obstacles but never give up. Empowering others has become my mission; I celebrate diversity and open doors through education and always encourage those who think they can't succeed. Working with a team believing in the empowerment of others gives me the drive to strive to give them something better. I feel a strong responsibility towards the community as it has provided me a platform to enrich myself as I achieve my vision of life."

Her career in the U.S. began as a pre-school teacher before being the Director of ASPIRA's Broward Division. Her commitment to education motivated her to raise thousands of dollars while working in ASPIRA to be given scholarships to numerous high schools. Then, in 2006 she was appointed to be the first Director of the Ana G. Mendez South Florida Campus. During her time with AGMU, she has expanded the organization's advocacy for access to higher education. Nazario-Cardona has also served as Chief Development Officer. "The Ana G. Méndez University has become the perfect platform to open doors to anyone who wants to progress. 'Access to high-quality education should not be just the privilege of some but the opportunity that should always be available to those who want to make their dreams come true,' Doña Ana G. Méndez once said. I have embraced this philosophy as part of my daily work, offering the necessary resources to the community to achieve education and knowledge as one of the most important tools that a human being can have." Syndia is a highly respected education and community leader because of her commitment, vision, and innovative leadership skills. Her focus is on student achievement, inclusion, and collegial capacity building with all stakeholders throughout the years. Ms. Nazario-Cardona has consistently shown great respect, support, and willingness to listen carefully and to honor the input of students, parents, teachers, support staff, and community stakeholders. Several organizations have recognized her for her work throughout the years: 100 Successful Women in Business' 100 Power Meter as one of the most influential Latino leaders in Washington DC, Maryland, and Virginia; and 100 Outstanding Women of Broward County. Years ago, she was appointed by Maryland's governor as part of the Higher Education Labor Relations Board and was featured in El Venezolano special edition magazine as a visionary.

"I encourage young professionals to believe that there are no limits; they must understand that to attain goals, it's important to work hard. History has proven the value of women in society; the

U.S. now has a woman vice-president. Remember that knowledge is power. Value your potential, and don't be afraid to take risks as you can find the power to strive within yourself. Surround yourself with other successful women that can help you with your growth. Finally, don't forget to live with passion while enjoying the opportunities life place in front of you. Believe in yourself!"

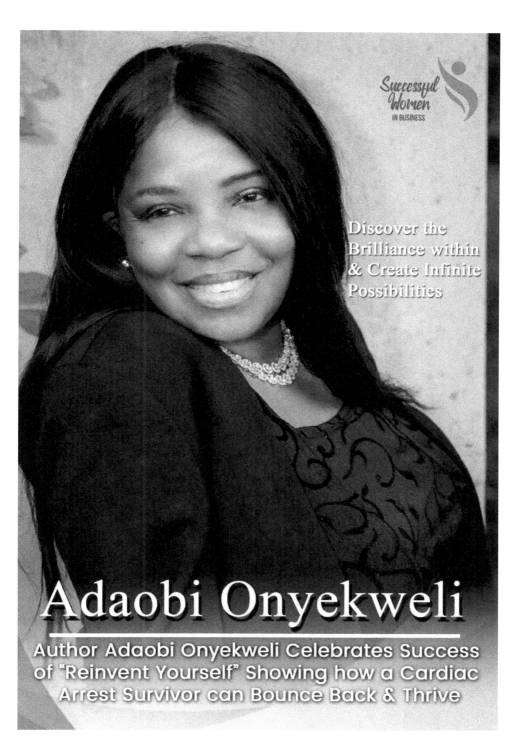

ADAOBI CORNELIA ONYEKWELI

How My Near-Death Experience Sparked the Biggest Career Change of My Life "When I let go of what I am, I become what I might be." -- Lao Tzu

I was born in Enugu, Nigeria to a family of 11. I had 9 siblings, and I was the 7th child. My earliest childhood memories were playing with my friends in the streets of Lagos. Coming from a middle-class family, I never lacked anything except the loss of my daddy at the age 11.

The 24th of December 2017, started like any normal day, except my life would undergo significant changes within 7 minutes of waking up. The ER doctor was white as a ghost. "There's a good chance she will never make it." he said. Now tell me, how does a family feel when they get told you might not make it? My siblings were in shock and family members had gathered to say their last goodbyes to me. "I had suffered a massive pulmonary embolism", the ICU doctor explained. There are big blood clots in the lungs. I had also suffered multiple organ failure, liver haematoma, and biliary sepsis and was brain dead. I managed to have survive after 2 months in a coma, barely able to see, sit, talk nor eat. After my discharge, I underwent serious rehabilitation, as I had to learn almost everything from scratch. As I lay in the ICU bed gazing at the beeping machine, I realized more than ever how fragile and short life is. Money and material things do not really matter at this stage.

I had to learn how to market and write my book. This resulted in my decision to open my own company, so that I could support the home rehabilitation of other people who had similar experiences with me. I am a Reinvention Coach and the author of the Amazon bestselling book, *Reinvent Yourself* and create infinite possibilities for your life. I have spoken in workshops and conferences. I have also won numerous awards, the first one being the Beautiful Survivor Award by LOANI. Through my organization, Put You First, I have been able to support women and families affected by their illnesses or just leaving the hospital with home rehabilitation support and emotional support to continue to thrive.

I had dreams but did not tell anyone nor try to achieve them due to not feeling good enough. I learned that I allowed myself to live with self-doubt all my life. I should have reached out for the right support. What challenges did you go through in your life? I realized that I had not been able to be true to myself. I am teaching women and young people that their voice matters. Women should make themselves part of the care priorities in their lives.

As I look back, I have learned 2 core lessons from surviving:

1. Life is too short and precious to waste in what you have or have not done. Know that when your life hangs in the balance, all that matters are people that you love and cherish.

2. All experiences in life matter and will be the backbone of who you will one day become.

I reckon it is up to us to make changes in our own life. As soon as I got out of the hospital, I got certified as a Public Speaker and put my story in a book. I started spreading the word, put up my website, and spoke at events to motivate others. You can do it; if you get stuck, then ask for help. Today, I support women to set up businesses and learn how to leave a legacy. The world needs you.

www.adaobionyekweli.com; thereinventioncoach on Instagram; linkedin.com/in/adaobi-onyekweli-729b1318b/; Adaobi Onyekweli on Facebook; www.putyoufirst.org

LENORA PETERSON-MUCLIN

As a child in the mid 60's I grew up in the inner city of Cleveland Ohio. I was the oldest of five siblings and faced many challenges due to my parents in ability to guide me. I learned many things independently and made multiple mistakes growing up. I had children at a young age and attended night school to obtain my high school diploma. During the early stages of my adult life, I worked hard to care for my children. I learned many trades and it allowed me to become a self-sufficient parent. As a volunteer at my church, I became more involved with my community. With the help of a mentor, I enrolled in community college that led me to work in a hospital within multiple departments for a span of 27 years. In addition to working at the hospital I became an entrepreneur as a coordinator and event planner.

I connected with other counties in community engagement by collaborating within a foreign country to learn how make our neighborhood and communities a better place to live and lean more about each other way of living. To keep teaching and training individuals on how to develop and serve in the community. With my online program I also want to keep recognition to individuals all around the world who help make a positive impact on building better communities.

Accomplishing many of my endeavors as an Ambassador, I have had the opportunity to learn about many cultures and to connect with amazing international people all over the world. As an African American woman thinking many of these opportunities were unattainable, I have learned with hard work and being persistent I am capable of so much. I used to have self-esteem issues. I always worried about what others thought about me. When I was young and growing up I tried to buy my friends friendship by always helping them and paying their way when we hung out.

My life mistakes assisted with me becoming the woman I am today. I learned I needed to push myself provide additional experiences for myself. It was time for me to network with individuals who allow me to elevate as Woman of God. I have endured multiplied challenges throughout life. I was diagnosed with a brain tumor in 2014. The tumor was affecting my vision and needed to be removed right away. After receiving surgery for the tumor removal, everyday challenges began. My speech, mobility, and concentration took a turn for the worst. I began to give up on life and suffer with severe depression. With prayer and God's guidance I overcame so many challenges.

Being heavily involved with community outreach, I am constantly assisting others. I help with providing everyday essentials for the less fortunate. Having the resources to establish programs that assist with improvement of our communities has made a huge impact.

My advice for woman is never give up on your dreams and goals. Stay persistent; keep your faith. Write down your goals and research what you will need to achieve them. Network with individuals. Make a plan; stick to it. Keep learning how to keep finding new strategies to help us to communicate in all cultures within" Diversity, Equity & Inclusion.

https://www.linkedin.com/in/petersonconsultingservice/

MIGUELAILLE PIERRE

We all have different goals that we would like to achieve, but it is how you are planning to achieve the goals. There are people with different desire to create something of their own, and still others who want to find ways to build it. Success can be fiddly, but we'll get through it if devoted to it.

Being determined---Think about what you want to do and ask yourself why! You need to have a reason why you want to do something to be able to succeed over the long-term or short-term goal. The Why is what is going to motivate you even when everything seems to be sinking apart.

Binding to your determination---It is easy to follow your goals once you commit to it and have the why. You need to completely invest yourself in your goals and be determined to see them through to be successful. If you do not commit to invest in your goals, someone else will get it done, and you will be watching them being successful at your own goals. If you want to do it, get it done instead of letting someone else to do it at their best interest.

Visualizing success---The more you see yourself doing something in your mind, the easier it will be to pick up a new step to get it done once you commit to it. Envision yourself living the type of lifestyle you desire and doing the things you want to do. Achievement is the key to your overall goal and accomplishment.

Be specific on your why---The why question should be your inspiration and your bigger purpose. The why is what drives you even when everything seems to be falling apart. People sometimes are always ready to know what you are doing but don't worry about why you are doing it. There should be a reason why.

Construct a positive environment for yourself.

Get connected to the places of where you are frequently in a positive mode. A depressing environment will suck the happiness and encouragement out of you. It is suggested to stay away from any negative environment.

Don't quit optimizing.

The process of developing, constructing, and reconstructing is part of your journey that never ends. Find ways to improve and make improvements; the more you practice and stick to your goals, the more you will succeed. Work on what you have to work on in everyday life and be greedy with your goals when wanting success. Break all the habits that will make you stop reaching out to your goals and stick to the steps that you have to take to accomplish your goal. If you find yourself struggling with any of the above steps, find a mentor who will be able to guide and help you through. Success does not come from outside; it comes from the inside.

Website: http://www.chaforem.com/

ANGELA POSILLICO

I was born and raised in Hackensack, New Jersey. I had an amazing family that guided me with wonderful advice throughout my childhood and my adult life. In my adult life, I was fortunate enough to work for several major companies, which taught me to grow and help me progress in my professional career. I also married a wonderful man who helped me pursue my goals in the professional world.

My dreams were to become a professional singer and perform in a major Broadway play.

My accomplishments are many. I had the opportunity to perform for President Nixon and performed in the East Coast Tour for Phantom of the Opera. I won the title of Mrs. New Jersey Globe in 1996 and was voted "Female Vocalist of the Year" in 1972 by the Reader's Digest Association. I Own my own company that empowers women.

The main thing that I have learned from my accomplishments----personal and professional---is never forget where you came from and the people that helped you climb the ladder of success. Success is never measured by what you do but by the amazing people that you surround yourself with.

My biggest failure is that I started my professional career too late and sometimes, never followed the advice of the individuals who tried to guide me on the correct path. What I learned from my mistakes is to never take anything for granted and learn to follow advice from the individuals that really care for you.

The biggest challenge that I faced was when my dad became seriously ill at a very young age. I had to learn to balance school, work, and trying to find a career path.

The biggest impact that I am making in my community is empowering so many young women that want to fulfill their dreams in modeling, business, and the entertainment industry. I have also worked with several charity organizations, where I was able to help the less fortunate and bring so many smiles to young children.

My advice to women reading this book is to learn something from everyone that is published. Experience is the best teacher. The one main tip that I can provide is never close your mind to new opportunities that may come your way. You can always learn new and successful ways at any age. The way to become successful is to know your worth, set your goals, and pursue your dreams!

http://www.mslatinainternational.com/

http://www.msinternationalworld.com/

RASHMI RAJ

Born in a small town in India, my father was a Govt. employee working as General Manager in Western Coalfields Limited, Nagpur; my mother was a home maker growing 3 kids along with managing her social life. We have 3 siblings in my family, 2 younger brothers – Mayank Rai & his wife Madhu - work for General Motors in Michigan, USA, and younger – Dr. Prashant Rai and his wife Dr. Bhanu Rai, Neurologists in Texas, USA.

My Childhood was very luxurious and pampered. I was a top scorer and Class Leader/Captain every year in a convent school, completed my Electronics Engineering, and pursued my MBA. I was made the DISCIPLINE COORDINATOR of entire Balaji Society hostel (Boys & Girls), comprised of 5 colleges and discipline coordinators of my own college, too, appointed by the college. I explored myself in many areas participating in Fashion shows competing in Intra college competitions. I was involved in creating the theme, designing the fashion costumes, and walking the ramp with my Cultural Coordinator in the college winning as 2nd runner-up.

My professional life with over 13 years of experience in Supply Chain Management & Project Management roles in UK & India. It is an enriching experience working with multinational companies in IT like IBM, Heineken UK, and Tech Mahindra. My vision and mission are to empower women and children to grow emotionally, financially, and support their families through my upcoming Organisation – ALVIRAGO Ltd

I am Founder & Director of AlVirago, Ltd, Chairperson of Ladies of All Nations International (Scotland), Country Director Scotland – International Youth Society focussing on UN SDG goals, Council Member of UK India Business Council of the Women's Indian Chamber of Commerce and Industry (WICCI), Top 10 Most Influential Indian Women 2019 in House of Lords (UK Parliament), Mahatma Gandhi Global Peace Award-2020(MGGPF-India), Human Excellence Award by IHRCCO (India), The Best Humanitarian Award in Scotland by ELS Edification Plus UK, Global Change Maker (UK) by LOANI, Women of the Year and Beauty on Earth International winner by The Republic of Women 2021, Princess Peace & Future Entity Leaders by LOANI & FEL(Egypt) 2021, She Inspires Me 2020 (UK), 100 Most Glamorous Women in The World by Elite International Beauties. I host TV shows and focus on International Conferences, Events, Fashion Shows and Awards, Campaigns, Allergy Awareness, projects like Save the Girl Child and Educate the Girl child in Scotland.

Be persistent no matter what stands in our way and move beyond what we can do; embrace our true potential. I have learnt to trust my instincts; when something just does not feel right back off and look in another direction. Failure is one of the main ingredients in success. You really do not know how good you are unless you really know how bad you have been! Manage personal & professional life. Manage community led initiatives and team. Face criticism and persistently work on improvements to get better every time. Live your dreams! Take that first step and jump. You will learn to survive and grow. Eventually, you will be the successful society role model! Be creative, optimistic, and determined with discipline and dedication!

REENU RAJ

Founder of RADANKS LTD UK. Dr. Raj believes a ray of happiness can be found even in the stormiest weather. You must aim for the target and focus on the final goal. Nothing can stop you once you start. Treasure even the small success. Dr.Raj's aim to help FIGHT DEPRESSION & RISE ABOVE FAILURE and ACHIEVE SUCCESS. The confidence and rigidness to achieve the dream must never fade from one; giving that motivation is her goal. She helps create a positive space that then helps people deal with their work-related stress and, therefore, increasing their productivity.

Dr. Raj's aim is to help FIGHT against domestic abuse. One in five people are known to suffer domestic abuse in silence and not to talk about it. There is always this hesitation to leave and walk; it feels easier to wear it as a tag on their card of life and continue to struggle. Her aim is to encourage them to share their pain and work though it to live in a healthier environment. Unseen domestic abuse is why it can be difficult to understand what is missing in one's life. Emotional Abuse is the most serious type which is rarely ever in discussion. She thinks her motivation and inspirational speech and concern will definitely change one's life to be successful.

As an expert on helping people deal with their emotional and work-related stresses, she increases their happiness and their resilience. Dr. Raj has been motivating people in different countries for more than nine years. Dr. Raj's sessions are designed to address the physical, mental, and emotional stress faced by people in different fields of work on a daily basis, especially in Domestic

Silence Abuse.

Dr Raj's technics are remarkably encouraging, innovative, motivating, high quality, and efficient by managing the mind and creating a positive attitude through smile, positive attitude, and other techniques. Her special style adds happiness to both personal and professional lives, thus bringing an overall change in the attitude and well-being of the people with whom she works.

For the last ten years she has been motivating and inspiring people to overcome all types of obstacles. She has helped youth to overcome drugs, and now they are pursuing their careers and life successfully. She has helped with a few family disputes, encouraged and empowered women to step out and make a mark for themselves in the world. She has helped people to speak up against Domestic Abuse as well Domestic Violence. She has motivated people to rise above their failure and achieve the success again in their business and from time to time has also helped people to overcome their depression.

Part of her vision is all about raising awareness for victims and survivors of domestic abuse. Her aim is to break the silence of victims of abuse. Her passion and mission are to continuously support victims/survivors of abuse giving them confidence and determination and freedom. NEVER LEAVE THE HOPE OF BRINGING HARMONY IN TOGETHERNESS.

Radankd is an International Consultancy Services Provider and Online Treaders.

07571474459 RADANKS.COM

SHAMILA RAMJAWAN

On the surface, I am a former Mrs. Johannesburg 2019 as well as an accomplished, renowned, formidable, and well-respected multiple global award winning entrepreneur. When I was 34 years old, my husband was struck with a sudden heart attack and passed on. This left me as a young widow to fend for myself and take care of my two young children.

I occupied senior management roles in various organisations and represented these organisations at Board level. However, having worked with communities for over a decade, I realised there was a dire need to research the menstrual cup as a sustainable solution for menstruation because impoverished girls miss school for up to 7 days in a month. I launched PrincessD Menstrual Cup which is reusable for ten years, a cost-effective, eco-friendly and hygienic product. To date, I have changed the lives of thousands of school girls, globally by "keeping girls in school".

The challenging entrepreneurial journey thus far, has been rocky yet extremely humbling at the same time. I confirm that I have respect for any person who decides to invest in their own venture. The specific experiences during this journey cannot be justified briefly but if I had to mention the highlight, I would say that it is knowing that I am making a positive impact whilst chasing my dreams.

Serving humanity has earned me an Honorary Doctorate of Humanitarianism from the Global International Alliance (GIA), USA. Affiliated with global organisations, I am the Africa

Chairperson for Ladies of All Nations International (LOANI UK and the Country Director for the International Youth Society (IYS).

Continually searching for the silver lining and making the best of any situation I find myself in, I started my own talk show "Red Corner Show" during Covid 19, where real life stories are shared by people from across the globe. Challenging situations and obstacles are a part of life, your story will help others to overcome their challenges too.

My most prized asset is the knowledge I gained over the years and I am a firm believer in the saying "knowledge is power". I've earned several qualifications and currently at the tail-end of my PhD. Acquiring knowledge through these qualifications and life experiences has equipped me to become a powerhouse entrepreneur. I am so passionate about learning that my current full time job is in academia where I am a Business Management Lecturer at the University of South Africa.

At heart, I have the nurturing characteristics of a mother but make no mistake that I can go head-to-head with the best of them in the boardroom as I strongly believe in the empowerment of women on all and any levels. All women have an inner lioness. The trick is to discover what brings it out in you and to never let that go.

I leave you with this: Never let anyone tell you that the sky is your limit because it is not. We are limitless.

Contact details:

Email: shamila@famramsolutions.com

Facebook:https://www.facebook.com/redcornershow

https://www.facebook.com/shamila.ramjawan/

YouTube:https://www.youtube.com/channel/UCWSvIoCqN-8V70F3NYIuanw/

Instagram:https://www.instagram.com/dr.shamila.ramjawan/?hl=en

https://www.instagram.com/princessdmenstrualcup/?hl=en

Website:www.princessdmenstrualcup.com

CECILIA ROKUSEK

"Live each day to the fullest and strive always to make a difference in the world and leave a piece of symbolic immortality behind you." These were the words my mother always lived by and inspired me to carry on with.

I, Cecilia Rokusek, grew up in the Midwest in the small Czech community of Tabor, SD. Culture and heritage were always very important to me. I am fluent in both Czech and Slovak, thanks to my parents. I always had a passion for education and learning new things. I always wanted to be a nutrition researcher, but my career path changed when I went into higher education. I was a professor, dean, provost, and president. I can honestly say that my time in higher education over 30 years was enriching and rewarding every single day. The students were the best part of each day. I am still in touch with so many of my students both in the U.S. and from aboard.

In 2008, I was appointed the Slovak Honorary Consul for the state of Florida. This position has afforded me the opportunity to do what I truly am passionate about---help people from my homelands in Central Europe. Most rewarding is the fact that I can work with students from Slovakia and help them in internships and study abroad programs. In 2018, I became the national president and CEO of the National Czech & Slovak Museum & Library in Cedar Rapids, IA. This has allowed me to continue my work with students from both the Czech and Slovak Republics. It has also allowed me to help preserve our rich Czech and Slovak cultures, celebrate these cultural stories, and help create new stories for the future. I want all people from all backgrounds to learn about their cultures and connect them to the rich stories of their ancestors. It is so important to cherish and preserve our immigrant past. I am proud to say that during my career I have established academic affiliations with institutions in other countries as well including Slovenia, Hungary, and South Korea. Although much of my career was in administration, I consider myself always a professor. Some of my proudest moments were when I co-founded a national Center for Disaster and Emergency Preparedness, one of only five such centers in the U.S. Through my executive positions in higher education, I have become skilled in grant writing, interdisciplinary health care research, and fundraising at the local, state, national, and international levels. I continue to be an international education consultant in the areas of higher education, interprofessional health care practice throughout the lifespan, primary care leadership, accreditation, and interprofessional geriatric care with focus on positive aging.

I have had many proud moments in my life, but some of the highlights have been receiving the Silver Medal for Distinguished Service from the Slovak Minister of Foreign Affairs in 2018 and the Woodrow Wilson Award for Leadership in Diplomacy in 2019 presented by the Slovak Ambassador to the U.S, Ivan Korcok, who currently serves as the Slovak Minister of Foreign Affairs. I was indeed blessed to have a great educational foundation that started in South Dakota where I attended Mount Marty College in Yankton, SD, for my undergraduate degrees in Dietetics and Communications. I then went on to the University of Nebraska in Lincoln where I was a Regents Scholar studying Human Nutrition. I received my Master of Science degree from UNL. I completed my doctorate in higher education administration from the University of South Dakota in Vermillion, SD.

My family, my culture, my passion for life, and my energy to make a difference make me want to get up each day. We can all make a difference in our world.

- 188 -

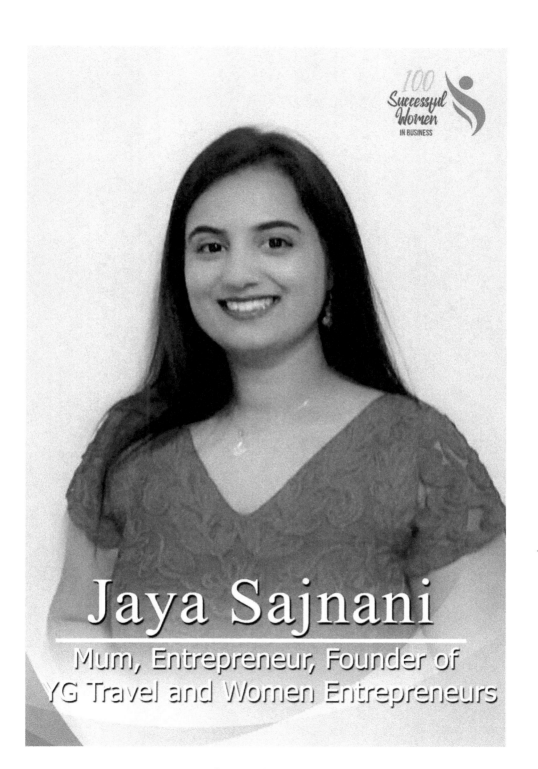

JAYA SAJNANI

Meet this Entrepreneur from London who is creating a mark and name in the male dominated industry. She provides transport solutions to many parents in London, works with the Education Institutions globally to provide educational tours, and enhances the experience of outdoor learning for the students. Alongside her social enterprise and NGO are helping and supporting many women in achieving their dreams. She has been awarded *The International Women Recognition Award 2019 – Entrepreneur* by the *Elite Club International Ltd at Delhi, India.* Nonetheless, she has been honored at the *House of Parliament, London* as *Young Entrepreneur 2019* and *Wonder Women 2019 Award*. Recently, Jaya Sajnani has made her mark in the industry by winning *The Business Transfer Specialists of the Year---London and Southeast England Prestige Award 2021*, and one of the Finalist at *2021 Amazon Everywoman in Transport & Logistic Awards.*

Jaya is originally from a small town but not less known called 'Anand' (also famous as Amul City) based in Gujarat, India. She belonged to the traditional Sindhi Family, very often known as Business Minds for decades by having high business spirit, which instilled the spark in her, too. She is a great example of women breaking the glass ceiling and daring to dream big and create a life of her own. She was born in a conservative Indian family, but her go-getter attitude and belief in herself has made her conquer the world on her own terms. She has built an organization which is creating a positive impact on society.

It was 2003 when she came to the UK to pursue her education post completing her graduation. She successfully completed her MBA-Finance from an esteemed University of West London, formerly known as Thames Valley University. Her qualification list added Public and Logistic Transport Manager qualification from OCR Oxford, Cambridge, and RSA examinations.

Like many women, Jaya left corporate life because the jobs just did not inspire her anymore. Starting a business allowed her to find meaning and gave her the ability to leave behind a legacy that she is very proud of. Upon asking the questions on the challenges and failure, she said, *"Failure is just a part of the process, and we have to start teaching people not to be afraid of failing. If you have tried something and it doesn't work, then just try something else. Get up and start over again, but this time you will not be starting from zero; you will start from the experience which you have got from the previous adventure!"* The biggest lesson I have ever learned is patience and perseverance are the keys to success. My favorite business tool or resource is my values - I do not go for any deal or act on anything if my gut feelings are saying otherwise. *"You can not change the direction of the wind, but you can always adjust the sails to reach your destination."*

She is also committed towards social responsibility to help and support women with their dreams. She has established a non-profit organization called "Women Entrepreneurs" which provides the platform where women help other women to start their own business, encourage each other, and take their business to the next level. A team of expert women in different fields of business support and encourage other women to pursue their own dreams.

Website: https://ygtravel.co.uk/about/

NADIA SANCHEZ

Nadia Sanchez is a business administrator, MBA, and specialist in human rights and political economy. She has worked in international development organizations, such as the Inter-American Development Bank IDB and the Organization of American States OAS (Washington D.C). Currently a businesswoman, entrepreneur, philanthropist, and international speaker, she serves as president and founder of the SHE IS Foundation, a model of economic empowerment and social inclusion for women and girls, one of the organizations of greatest impact in Latin America and Colombia benefiting more than 10,400 women and girls in the region, where she also led the Tour for reconciliation seeking to unite an entire country. She was Director for Latin America of the Women Economic Forum WEF (2019 and 2020). She was a professor at the Pontificia Universidad Javeriana in Bogota in the areas of social innovation and entrepreneurship and is a member of the committee of women leaders of the Americas of the OAS and the Documentary Center Foundation of Spain. Her career has been decorated in more than 10 countries with lectures in more than 15 countries around the world, recognized as one of the most influential and impactful entrepreneurs by the World Bank (2017) and the White House Washington (2015) among others. She has led in Colombia the initiatives of gender equity and good practices for the private sector with the first book in production; she is one of the most influential leaders with her purpose and struggle for peace building and human rights, gender equality, and generation of opportunities for education that reduce poverty gaps, signing historic agreements, such as the one made with the NASA

Space Center, among others supporting girls in vulnerable situations accessing STEAM careers, a foundation established in Costa Rica and Spain.

Her AWARDS include the following: Policarpa Salavarrieta Order and Merit Decoration, granted by the Congress of the Republic of Colombia, March 8, 2021; Woman Who Inspires around the World, Government of Egypt, National Council for Women in Egypt. March 2020;

International Social Leader, Women of the year 2020, Houston Council Member. Houston, Texas USA. March 2020; The Global Democracy Award given by The Washington Academy of Political Arts and Sciences, (WAPAS), Washington D.C 2019; Woman of the Decade for Peacebuilding by the Women Economic Forum 2019; Global Award given during her participation in New Delhi, India: "ICONIC WOMEN NURTURING A CULTURE & ECOSYSTEM FOR INNOVATION" Iconic woman around the world, awarded for building innovative ecosystems for women for two consecutive years. New Delhi - India. (2016 – 2017 - 2018); UNDP Regional Call for Proposals "Experiences that make a difference: Gender Equality and Women's Economic Empowerment in the Territories". April 2018; 4th place in the prestigious "IDEAS FOR ACTION" program of Wharton School and World Bank (Top 10) Washington D.C.; Third place Schmidheiny Award in Social Innovation. Viva Idea Costa Rica

Woman entrepreneur 2017 by the OAS, YABT, WORLD BANK and PEPSICO; selected and awarded a scholarship by the UN for the "Women for Peace" program at University for Peace Costa Rica 2017; Young Woman Leader CAF 2016; National Award for Social Responsibility, as a Woman Manager of Equality, PROBONO PERU Foundation 2016; awarded by the Mayor's Office of Cajica,

Colombia, and by the Municipal Council in September 2014 and February 2016 as "Woman of the Year".

JANET SMITH WARFIELD

Fifty years ago, Dr. Janet Smith Warfield had a mystical experience. It wasn't something she was trying to have. She didn't know what to call it. She just knew she had experienced a sudden understanding and clarity.

Nothing outside her changed. All that changed was her understanding of her external world. Suddenly, she was looking at everything through new eyes.

She had to tell others. No one understood. How could she use analytical, divisive words to communicate a unifying, holistic experience? It was like trying to wash dishes using a broom. Mystical experiences have always been called "ineffable." They cannot be talked about accurately.

Janet began playing with words, discovering all the creative ways they structure our experiences. She wrote poetry ,stories, journaled and she questioned. Words were illusions, dancing at a masked ball. They were fingers pointing at the moon. They were not the moon.

Alfred Korzybski wrote, "The map is not the territory."

There is this unifying, holistic, enlightening, transformational experience that has been experienced by people all over the planet from the beginning of time. It has been named by different people in different ways: "salvation," "enlightenment," "satori," "awakening," "I am aware." As soon as anyone tries to talk about it, they are creating a conceptual map of the experience. Each map is different, and the map is not the territory. The words are not the experience.

Socrates used questions. Jesus used parables. Buddhists teach the Noble Eightfold Path. Zen Buddhists use koans.

For fifty years, Janet has had many holistic, creative, right-brain transformational experiences. For 22 years, she practiced rigorous, left-brain law. Throughout her life, she has been playing with human-created language and honing her people skills. Out of this, an art form has emerged that Janet calls "Word Sculptures." Word Sculptures uses words in atypical ways to shift people into experiences beyond words, transforming turmoil into inner peace.

When we change our words, we change our world; our emotions change, our actions change, and our relationships change. If we all understood what we do with words, together, we would be astonishingly powerful and effective in co-creating the dynamic, respectful, peaceful, powerful, prosperous planet we all need to survive and thrive.

Credentials:

- Graduate of Swarthmore College and cum laude graduate of Rutgers School of Law, Camden.

- Studied with Barbara Marx Hubbard, Jean Houston, Andrew Harvey, Joanna Macy, Ken Wilber, T Harv Eker, Mark Victor Hansen.

- Author of Amazon Best Seller, *Shift: Change Your Words, Change Your World.*

- 2008 Indie Next Generation Book Award Winner – Best New Age Non-Fiction.

- Continental Who's Who's 2015 Most Prominent Professional in the Field of Consciousness Education.

- International Association of Top Professionals (IAOTP) Top Professional in the Field of Consciousness Education (2016-17).

- Woman of the Year (Turning Point Media, 2017)

- International Association of Top Professionals (IAOTP) Top Female Motivational Speaker of the Decade (2020)

- Founder, Planetary Peace, Power, and Prosperity Legacy Foundation, Inc. (2020)

- America's Most Influential Women: (International Who's Who, 2021)

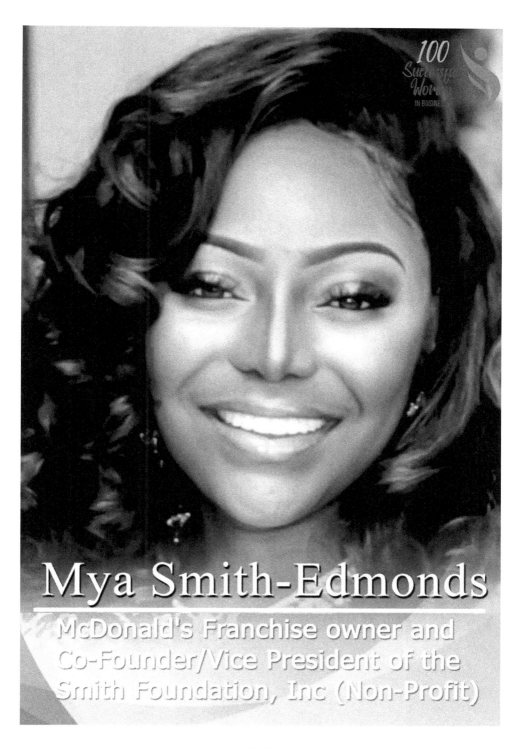

- 206 -

MYA SMITH-EDMONDS

McDonald's Franchise Owner (9 Restaurants), Co-Founder/Vice President of the Smith Foundation, Inc (Non-Profit), Real Estate Developer & Investor, Amazon #1 Best Selling Author God Will Do Exceedingly, Abundantly, Above All You Could Hope, Ask or Think... Ephesians 3:20

As a child, I wanted to make a difference. At 11, I earned my allowance by doing chores, making excellent grades, being respectful, babysitting, and doing great in sports. I used my allowance to send to other countries to help children needing food, healthcare, clothes, water, etc. I needed to be EXTREMELY successful if I was going to make a difference in people's lives. I decided to be an Entrepreneur/Business Owner. You already know that there is a LARGE gap, FILLED with obstacles, trials, tribulations, let downs, unmet expectations, no's, sacrifices, change, pain, struggle, etc. that take place from the moment you DECIDE what you want to the time it ACTUALLY happens... IF IT HAPPENS...

I decided to be a McDonald's Franchise Owner of multiple locations...Dreaming Big. It takes the SAME Faith process to believe for a loaf of bread that it takes to believe to OWN the Entire Bakery, so I put my Faith to work. Faith is an ACTION. McDonald's wants applicants to possess key attributes: Financial Wisdom, People Skills, Assets/Cash Flow, Excellent Credit, Reputable Character, Astute Knowledge of the Business, Operational Excellence, Customer Satisfaction, Profitable Results, Manage/Develop People, etc. If you are Focused/Consistent, the program could take 24 months--otherwise up to 5+ years (no guarantees on timelines or approval) I'm very Focused/Determined! I completed my training, classes, results, etc. in 12 months. I didn't just finish in 12 months. I MASTERED EVERY AREA from achieving the Highest Rankings, Grades & Awards on each step, achieved Ray Kroc Award (Only for the Top 1% performing leaders), broke records, built business and developed people, financial wisdom, assets, excellent credit, etc...I was SURE I'd be approved Immediately! Guess what? I WAS NOT!! I heard responses from "you are not in the program" to "we didn't receive the documentation of all your progress from the previous corporate consultant (several times I had to start over)" to "you'll need to relocate (moved 7 times)". I was 4 years in frustrated and devastated because I was doing everything I was supposed to do. This is the moment, where we all could possibly get STUCK in our journey to success. When you are DOING EVERYTHING, yet "NOTHING" is happening, and it seems that NOTHING is working. This is the DEFINING MOMENT. What you do now will determine EVERYTHING at this moment in your journey, I encourage you to do what I did: "PRESS ON" in Faith & PUSH (Pray Until Something Happens)!

Not only did I become a McDonald's Owner; but God Blessed Me Far Beyond what I could HOPE, Ask or Think! Ephesians 3:20 After only 7 years, I Own 9 McDonald's Restaurants. I made history in becoming the First/Only, African American Next Generation Owner in the Indianapolis Region. I received many awards... Trailblazer (NAWBO) National Association of Business Owners, Galore Distinction, featured on the COVER of many magazines, and featured on The Billboard in New York City – Times Square. I've been able to be a Blessing to so many others through our Smith Foundation, Inc. where we've awarded over $108,000 in

Scholarships in the last 2 years. I've received The Humanitarian Award, Recognized by Global Trade Chamber as one of the 100 Most Successful Women Around the World in Business, featured In/On the COVER of Global Trade Chamber Business Magazine, recognized by CORE Magazine as a CORE 100 Most Influential Blacks Today, recognized by our United States Congresswoman Sheila Jackson Lee as "Woman of the Year" from Ladies of Great Purpose & Positive Black Male Association, awarded a Proclamation, declaring an official day be named after me, the "Myasha "Mya" Smith-Edmonds Day" by our Mayor Sylvester Turner; and much more...

If I had given up when I did everything required within 12 months or when I had to start over several times or during one of the 7 moves, I would NOT have experienced God's BEST for my life. Jeremiah 29:11, 1 Corinthians 2:9 NEVER QUIT!!! God is NOT a respecter of person, what he does for one in principle; HE WILL DO FOR ALL! Just like it happened for me. IT CAN & WILL HAPPEN FOR YOU! After Persevering under Trial, Trusting God, Never Giving up and having Stood the Test, you "WILL" receive the Crown (Victory) God promised (James 1:12).

Poonam Soni

Founder Poonam Soni Jewelry
Pioneer in exclusive luxury handcrafted jewelry and accessories

- 212 -

POONAM SONI

Poonam Soni is a luxury jewelry brand from India founded by the designer in 1989. Having broken through a tightly closed and conservative Indian jewelry market against all odds, Poonam Soni deservedly got to be known as the pioneer of designer jewelry in India.

She broke all existing norms in the male dominated industry and launched path breaking collections which focused on design and aesthetics rather than investment. She incorporated unheard of materials in fine gold and diamonds to give a unique look, like leather, shells, fabric, and semi-precious, colorful stones. Her jewelry made a statement, was bold, striking, and multidimensional. It caught the eye of the discerning customer who was hungry for unique styles, and soon Soni had established her brand.

She was wooed nationally and internationally and featured in magazines all over the world. Prince Albert 2 of Monaco invited her for a global tour where her jewelry brooch was auctioned by Lord Mark Poltimore of the auction house Sothebys at the second highest price. Mark Jamet of the LVMH group invited her to showcase at the opening of the Incredible India event in Paris. Michael Kors discovered her in Vogue, endorsed her Collection, and introduced her to Linda Fargo, the stylish gatekeeper of Bergdorf and Goodman in New York.

Poonam Soni created a legacy of jewelry inspired by art and architecture and her collections with hand painted art canvases 'Monochromes' became world famous. Gaudi Revived received

Spanish patronage and authentication. BBC Jet, the luxury channel from London, flew down for a day to interview this designer who was sought after by the collector of fine gems. Coffee table books wrote extensively about her, and the Black Book labelled her "Designer of the Collector". The Tahitian government chronicled her work in magazine. Soni's collaborations with royal families, Valentino, Rolls Royce, BMW, Judith Leiber, and many more put her on the world map.

As Soni's growth was like a tornado the negativity, and competition was equally powerful. However, keeping herself spiritually inclined through her Buddhist philosophy, this Designer emerged to grow steadily and surely with a very loyal customer for whom Soni designed custom jewelry. Soon she was the most awarded designer in the country with national and luxury awards and felicitation adorning a room in her opulent flagship store. The brand is also the recipient of the Deebeers Millionaire Award 2000 received by Soni's daughter Kriti by Oppenheimer himself at the Louvre in Paris. Her younger daughter has worked as VP in Ralph Lauren accessories in New York. The legacy is strong.

In a devastating economy, Soni's brand stands stable through a virtual business and a new break through concept of reviving customers old locker jewels into a new look called 'Metamorphosis.' In 2021 look out for Soni's edge cutting new Collection 'Animal Farm Revived' based on George Orwell's satire where Soni's message is clear to humanity. It's now time to live in peace and harmony.

Website: www.poonamsoni.com

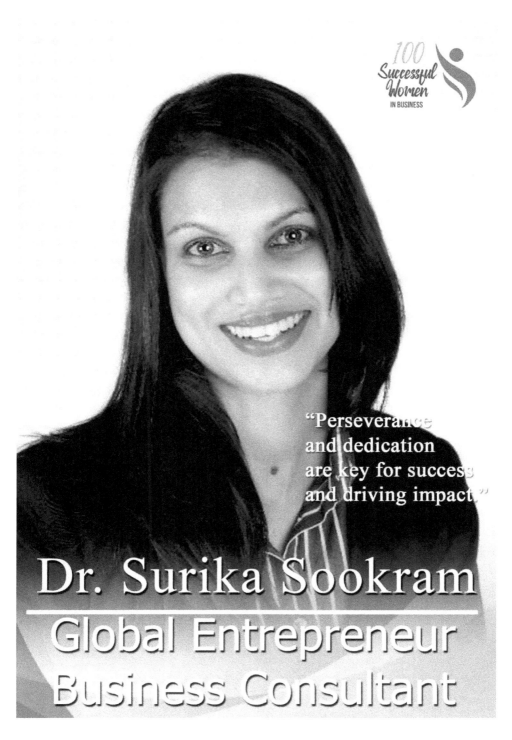

- 216 -

SURIKA SOOKRAM

My passion for serving my profession and society has informed many of my career decisions and has allowed me to grow as a leader and contributor to society. Creativity and literature have been characteristics that have been instilled in me at an early age. This was evident when I won a silver medal in the Shankar's International Award in India, an award for the categories of creativity and literature. It was at this stage that my love for literature and research had developed. I was awarded a bursary for academic excellence by a software company in South Africa and obtained an IBM excellence award for my Master's degree. I also hold a Ph.D. degree from the University of KwaZulu-Natal focusing on strategy and entrepreneurship. My passion for enabling the economy through entrepreneurs led me to focus my research on the implementation of information, communication, and technology strategy in small and medium enterprises in both local and international entrepreneurial businesses. This research resulted in the recommendations of policies and training programs to be implemented to resolve core issues being faced by SMEs.

I have extensive experience leading multi-functional teams in mid-cap to large-cap organizations. In my many corporate roles, I have gained extensive leadership experience, such as a General Manager for an internet services provider that operates in Africa. My prior roles include being a part of South Africa's Top 40 JSE-listed and large blue-chip companies such as MTN and KPMG.

I take great pride in running a successful organization. These skills are evident in my role as CEO of Mbono Advisory which I co-foundered in 2016. This business focuses on the development of SME content to aid the successful creation of start-ups. In this role, I was fortunate to have been consulted by a global keynote entrepreneur that is based in Silicon Valley.

I am passionate about community development and woman empowerment. My objective is to utilize my skills and experience to drive social and economic empowerment initiatives in SMEs and women-owned businesses This objective is aimed at educating and capacitating women to lead social change. I live by this by leveraging my strengths and Ph.D skills and by mentoring and coaching other entrepreneurial women globally in technology and business start-ups to achieve growth. This mentoring and coaching drive is achieved through organisations, such as Cherie Blair Foundation for Women, Tony Elumelu Foundation, and the National Mentorship Movement. My journey of learning and accomplishment has earned me a placement in prestigious organisations, such as the Golden Key International Honour Society, only accessible to individuals who finish in the top 15% of the university's academic class. I am also a member of the Institute of Directors South Africa. I believe in staying authentic to what makes you distinctive. Hard work, perseverance, and continually bringing your passions to the table no matter where you are seated are key ingredients for being successful and impactful.

DEE THOMPSON

My prayer is that this book transforms your life and inspires you to be great in all that you do.

I was born and raised in Gary, Indiana, the baby of 5 in a two-parent traditional household. I was extremely close to my dad. He taught me life lessons about tenacity and positive thinking during every conversation; I listened intently. At 12 years old I lost my dad due to gun violence. Upon arriving home from a family vacation during the wee hours in the morning, my dad left to drop an uncle off at his home 4 blocks away. As they were unloading luggage from the trunk, he forcefully became the getaway car for a robbery that had just occurred on the same corner. His body was found a few days later.

Losing my dad at such a young age left me devastated and hopeless and in desperate search of purpose. By the time I was 17 years old, I graduated high school, had a baby as a single-parent, and was caretaker for my mom who had several strokes. I was failing at life and in desperate need of life support!

I began to contemplate my dad's words, "Never give up on your dreams." I cried out to God as I envisioned my future and propelled my life into one I so desired. I subsequently married my best friend Loran Thompson and relocated to Florida several years later. We had 2 children together, are now grandparents, and have been married for 32 years.

My passion was to help those unable to find purpose by harnessing their God-given gifts and talents and turning them into profitable pursuits via one of my signature coaching programs. I knew that was something special, a unique gift and ability to skillfully dig deep into other's lives and help them extract purpose thus (The Purpose Doctor). I knew that the discovery of one's true self would ultimately shift the trajectory of their lives as it had in my own life. I teach others that when you can't find your path in life, don't follow the crowd, follow purpose; it will give you direction and lead to undeniable private and public success.

I authored a book, "Purpose Never Dies" It's alive in you because what's lying dormant inside of you is awaiting its birth. Purpose didn't die with life's tragedies; rise up and shine!

I've empowered my community over the last 20 years by leading and serving. I've branded company within the marketplace by hosting major events, including one of the very last Barack Obama Presidential Lifetime Achievement Awards Ceremonies honoring 31 people, my signature events, "The Best Coaches in the U.S.", and "Coffee, Tea, and Dee" in South Florida. I am hosting the GIA Honorary Doctorate Degree in Humanitarianism Ceremony for 24 individuals on 09/11/21, highlighting humanitarian efforts.

I have transformed the lives of thousands of individuals, celebrities, businesses, ministries, etc. as an Internationally Certified Life Coach, Relationship Coach (filmed segment for Bravo TV), Minister, and Chaplain all on purpose!

Website:

http://DeeThompsonSpeaks.com/

Evangelia Vassilakou

BA in Philosophy MA in Applied Linguistics Hellenic American University.

EVANGELIA VASSILAKOU

Being a child of a divorced family, I, Evangelia Vassilakou, grew up mostly in a cold and impersonal family environment. Affection, care, and parental tenderness had been eclipsed by a "family vacuum". I never had the chance to share my inner thoughts and frustration moments with my parents being engrossed in their personal problems. Book therapy was the source of my mental health and management of feelings. My mantra was "when the universe seems to betray you, books can be your best friend". From a young age I was magnetized by the charm of books, the wisdom they hide, and the perfect linearity of printed letters. These special moments of my literacy formed the biggest dreams of mine. To compensate for the icy family surroundings, the world fantasized in my eyes as an amiable, secure, and loving environment for people of all ages and nationalities. I visualized myself as an awakener-educator, endorsing character ethics, enlightening hordes of student populace, and inspiring generations for a good cause. I dreamed of restoring the broken mirror of my microcosm by eliminating the ugliness of the macrocosm.

Years later, I entered the American College of Greece and got my Bachelor of Arts degree in Philosophy. Afterwards, I started flirting with the "demons of my perfectionistic mind" of constant professional development. Despite my family's opposition to my pursuing a Master of Arts degree in Applied Linguistics, I realized that knowledge is power per se and being married or having three children should only be a challenge rather than an obstacle. It was that inner inquisitive nature of mine that listened to the voice of further success in life.

However, success is not a polished notion as it entails failures. We are the sum of our mistakes and I experienced a plethora of challenges before becoming a graduate of Salutatorian laurels. My financial vulnerabilities and my family responsibilities made my success path foggy and treacherous. I made the mistake of being too overwhelmed by this journey to a higher degree. I can confess neglecting spending more precious family moments, socializing with beloved friends, skipping meals, or photocopying my university books to avoid spending money, and staying sleepless for days to meet assignment deadlines. Nevertheless, I learned that mistakes are an integral part of success.

Today, I herald the year of 2021 with 2 academic degrees, a salutatorian medal, 2 Honorary Doctorates, 14 awards, 50 national and international talks in 11 countries, 20 ELT article publications, 6 conference proceedings, 4 journal article publications in peer-reviewed scientific journals, one chapter in an edited book published by Cambridge Scholars Publishing (UK), many memberships in human rights organizations, and many social media appearances-online interviews, podcasts, article and book dedications-with some exceeding 2.000 views internationally.

The magic of success is to believe in you, love what you do, act, and share. Success is nothing if not shared with the people that trust you enough to be imbued with the metamorphic ability of YOUR success colors.

- 228 -

BARONESS ANGELIKA VON CANAL-CHRISTIE

How discovering my 'Inner Hero' changed everything.

There comes a time in your life when you are at a crossroad and your Soul knows exactly what to do, yet your mind keeps you stuck because it's afraid of the unknown. I know all about crossroads!

It all started when I was 12 years old at my boarding school where a nun cursed me that I'll never have an honorable life because I disobeyed her rules; this spell became deeply imprinted in my subconscious mind. It took decades until I realized why I was the one to leave my marriage, and other relationships out of fear that I was not good enough or didn't deserve to be happy. After two divorces, I married my second husband again. After ten years of soul searching, self-discovery, and professional studies in Self Development and Relationship dynamics, I knew that I could help women to prosper, too. My soul knew it, yet my mind argued that after 30 years of successfully managing two businesses including my Health and Healing Center in the Bahamas, it was time to become a "Lady of Leisure": take it easy, have fun, and just be involved in the lives of my five children and nine grandchildren.

I'll never forget one fateful early morning; I was walking on the beach after another restless night. I challenged God to give me a clear sign what "HE" wants from me in the second part of my life. I just had to know. I argued out loud into the open sky whether it was too late for me and if I could still bring my gift out into the world in an even bigger way.

My indecision tormented me; I felt as if a blade of steel turned in my heart until the pain was unbearable and I cried out loud: "God stop this pain!" Suddenly, a wave of softness washed through me and took every bit of pain out of my body. Then, powerful energy surged through me from the top of my head into my womb. I felt my knees hitting the powdery white sand. I never forget that moment when, through streams of tears, powerful images appeared from deep within me: a black stallion as a battle horse and a silver winged mare. I knew immediately that my soul gifted me with those two images. I call them "My Inner Hero" Both images turned into powerful tools for courage and healing which have come when I need to take inspired action.

I do not remember how long I was kneeling in the sand beside the ocean, yet from that moment on I knew that I was not done yet, and that I had received the mandate to inspire, influence, empower, and liberate the woman of a certain age who feels trapped in her mind or a relationship. Are you that woman? Let me guide you to experience the joy and fulfillment as the unapologetic and magnificent woman that you truly are.

Websites:

www.baronessangelika.tv

http://www.angelikachristie.com/

Stepping Out of My Comfort Zone
Dr. Randi D. Ward
Educator, Author, Visionary Book Writing Coach, Master Editor, Multi-award Recipient

- 232 -

RANDI D. WARD

"Believe. Don't dream big; dream bigger. The sky is the limit so reach for the stars." (Dr. Randi D. Ward) www.randidward.com

I have spent my life rediscovering who I am, who I want to be, and what I want to achieve. As a young girl, I was an excellent student but lacked self-confidence and hid in the shadows of successful people. When I started teachers' college at Marshall University, I decided to step out of my comfort zone and become the woman I dreamed I could be. The next four years enabled me to grow and overcome difficult challenges. In graduate school, I met my husband and "earthly savior", who convinced me anything I wanted was possible.

Career #1 began in 1971 as a language arts/gifted teacher in West Virginia and Georgia. After 37 years, I retired in 2008 but discovered my career dreams had not been completely fulfilled. In 2011, I challenged myself as a teacher again during a three-month ESOL position with young adults in Cairo, Egypt. Little did I know the second revolution would begin one week after my arrival. Deeply touched by my experiences there, I began Career #2 with my first book *Because I Believed in Me (My Egyptian Fantasy Came True)*. I now write in many genres and am a motivational blogger, international speaker, and YouTuber. In 2020 I became an International Best-Selling Author in *Quarentena and Beyond*. My writing entertains, inspires, and educates. Career #3 began because of a WPN tele-conference call with a guest coach. My husband sadly died on December 15, 2019; I was deeply depressed. I had lost my life focus. This call spoke to my heart and soul. July 1, 2020, I became a Harmony Life and Holistic Emotional Intelligence Coach and an NLP Practitioner. Career #3 is now as a book writing coach and editor. I am currently the editor for three magazines and individual books, including this book you are reading.

Taking risks has blessed me with over 50 prestigious awards/ honors—professionally and personally. Between 2013-2016, I opened two Egyptian schools with Egyptian partners there. Both closed due to circumstances beyond our control. I do not consider them failures-only business lessons for future growth. Personally, I have had to find creative ways to keep walking due to serious knee problems. All my life since age 15 years, doctors have told me I am a miracle to be able to walk. I just consider myself as a stubborn woman who never gives up.

Taking risks in our lives can be intimidating and frightening. However, we must take risks to succeed. Sometimes we fail, but if we do not take a chance, we fail before we even begin. Our whole life perception changes when we look at our challenges as new, exciting adventures in learning. Risk taking is opening oneself to change, accepting the need for change, and taking the steps necessary to accomplish this change. It enables us to pursue our goals/dreams and to discover new talents/abilities. It makes us feel powerful/ proactive---putting us in charge of our futures instead of waiting for something to happen which is out of our control.

Don't dream big; dream BIGGER. Never give up.

INDIA WHITE

I am the ninth out of ten children and am originally from Sarasota, Florida. As an honor roll student at the age of 16, my mother kicked me out of the house on Christmas Eve. As a homeless youth, I obtained 18 scholarships, including a full ride from Bill Gates to attend the University of Florida, where I majored in math.

I became a math teacher and was nominated 2 times for Teacher of the Year. I obtained a Masters in Ed. Leadership and was promoted to a National Ed Consultant. I graduated with my Doctorate in Ed. Leadership, using my findings as a professional speaker on content regarding equity.

My dreams include being a philanthropist while increasing my impact as a believer in Jesus Christ to help people find their purpose in life. I aspire to coach thousands of leaders.

I'm humbled to be 3 times graduate from the University of Florida, a professional speaker, and a national education consultant that has evolved into an expert on equity. I've been privileged to publish 3 dozen books. Further, I've coached internationally and launched a "Coaching Rockstars" Course! I learned you can overcome anything; as long as you persist, you will overcome.

I learned that failures are learning lessons. They do not define who you are. They build you and without failure, you can't have true success. My mistakes remind me that I am simply not perfect, and that there's always room for growth and improvement.

I lost four family members in the span of a month at the age of 16, including my brother as a homeless youth, and I lost my sister, mother, and father in a span of 3 years.

I love coaching and mentoring women, entrepreneurs, and students into overcomers via my Coaching Rockstars Course and as a speaker! I helped raise multi-millions of dollars in scholarships for at-risk youth.

Never let anyone define who you are evolving into. Let God define your purpose and keep him at the center of everything you do!

Pray to the Lord and be honest.

Get a TEAM---It takes a village!

Celebrate you; don't be so hard on yourself!

Success is inevitable to everyone. You must imagine it, speak it, believe it, and then pursue it with all you've got!

Website: https://www.india-white.com/

DAWN AIRHART WITTE

I am Dawn Airhart Witte originally from Ohio and have lived in Los Angeles for thirty-four years. I am the proud mom of two amazing daughters; raising them has been the most rewarding experience of my life. Now that my daughters are adults, I have turned that same passion for loving and nurturing children everywhere into the foundation I started called The Desire to Inspire Foundation. I want to inspire people everywhere to live their happiest and most fulfilling lives. I am a certified life coach and one of the first things I learned was about the Universal Law of Reciprocity. This law states that whatever is sent out into the universe, either in thoughts, emotions, or actions will manifest outcomes in our own life. Like Karma, what we give, we receive. When we keep our giving and receiving in balance, there is no limit to the many blessings that will come our way. Being able to touch another's life in love and kindness is what I feel called to do. One of my favorite quotes is by Ralph Waldo Emerson which says, "To know even one life has breathed easier because you have lived, this is to have succeeded." This is how I define success.

Since I started my foundation and business, I have made many mistakes, but I do not believe in failures unless we give up. Sometimes we think something is supposed to happen a certain way in a certain time frame, and when it does not happen that way, we lose hope or think that we have failed. When we are so grounded in our purpose, giving up is not an option. When I look at all my "mistakes," I am able to see that I was being redirected in a better and more beautiful way.

Over the past four years I have spent nearly four months in five countries in Africa. We have delivered nearly 2500 "Little Books of Be..." to children in Ghana, Uganda, Sierra Leone, Rwanda, Kenya, and the US. We have drilled three boreholes to provide clean water, held health screenings, built a sick bay, performed a wharf clean-up, moved our girls in Sierra Leone to a home and provided beds, and met basic food and medical needs for hundreds of children. We have spoken to them all about finding their gifts and sharing them with the world.

My advice to everyone is to believe in themselves and believe in their dreams. I write about the power of choosing to be seven words to live your happiest and most fulfilling life. Everyone's life has challenges and being STRONG will help you persevere. Understand the importance of being GRATEFUL for your life; you are here for your own special reason. Be INSPIRED so you may see the beauty and wonder each day while you share your great talents with others. The world needs your unique gifts. Realize that kindness and love are currencies far more valuable than money. LOVE and KINDNESS are our highest currency. Always know to be true to who you are and GENUINE about who that is because there will only ever be one you and you are a gift to the world. Finally, choose to be HAPPY because happiness puts out a special energy into the world that brings about even more joy as it spreads.

Website:

https://desiretoinspirefoundation.org/

ACKNOWLEDGEMENT

This book would not have been possible without the support, ideas and promotion from the global organizations that are committed to helping so many people in so many countries, The Global Trade Chamber, The 100 Successful Women in Business Network and LOANI - Ladies of All Nations.

We would like to acknowledge the help of all the people involved in this project and more specifically, to the authors and reviewers that took part in the review process. Without their support, this book would not have become a reality.

We thank each one of the contributors from so many walks of life and so many nations, for sharing their unique stories, challenges, triumphs, and their wisdom. We also would like to acknowledge that the remaining contributors of the "100 Most Successful Women around the world", will be featured in volume two.

Second, the editors wish to acknowledge the valuable contributions of the reviewers regarding the improvement of quality, coherence, and content presentation of chapters.

We are grateful to the authors, Maria Renee Davila MBA, Founder of the 100 Successful Women in Business Network and CEO of the Global Trade Chamber, as well as Professor Dr. Caroline Makaka Founder/CEO of Ladies of All Nations International.

A special thanks to these special ladies that have contributed in many ways to the success of this wonderful book. Dr. Randy Ward President/CEO/Founder at Randi D. Ward, Dr. India White Speaker,

Best Selling Author, Robbie Motter, CEO/Founder of Global Society for Female Entrepreneurs (GSFE) and Angela Covany, CEO/Founder of Havana Book Group LLC.

And finally, to the GTC Graphics Team for the beautiful design and layout of the covers and content of the book.

ABOUT THE AUTHORS

MARIA RENEE DAVILA, BBA, MBA

Maria-Renee is the CEO of the Global Trade Chamber, an international chamber helping entrepreneurs and companies start, grow, and explore new global markets, also is the Founder of the 100 Successful Women in Business Network that empowers, connects and recognizes women around the world. She is also an International Business Trainer and International Speaker. A Multi-award winner that has received public recognition from local, national, and foreign governments, Non-Public Organizations, and various multinational companies.

Past Board Member of Latin Women Business Organization. Business Professor in several Universities in Florida for over 10 years. Maria-Renee Davila, originally from Bolivia, is a proven international entrepreneur with extensive corporate experience and solid leadership skills. Maria-Renee Davila started her modeling career at the age of 12 and opening in her first company at 17, a Modeling, Etiquette & Protocol Academy. As the academy grew, new divisions opened, the academy expanded to a model agency, dance, beauty pageants and later a full event and video production company. Becoming one of the top agencies in the country. Past Co- Host for a National TV Show. Maria-Renee Davila has over 20 years of experience in operations of companies. She also has served as director for other companies and worked with Fortune 500 companies, where she provided consulting and resources enabling companies to succeed in local and international markets.

PROF. CAROLINE MAKAKA

Multi Award Winner Dr Caroline Makaka is the Founder/CEO of Ladies of All Nations International also known as LOANI which compromises of Beautiful Survivors World of Honors, United in Diversity Special Recognition Awards and Galaxy of Stars Young Inspirational Awards and LOANI Magazine. Caroline has been recognized by numerous & Prominent Bodies. She is a mother, Patron an Orphanage School in Africa, Board Advisor for Central Entrepreneur Capital Union, President of Aesthetics International UK , Save the Girl Child Ambassador.

Global Peace Ambassador, Board Advisor, VIE Equality & Diversity International Ambassador, Advocate for Women, Entrepreneur, Philanthropist, Community Developer, Charity Worker, Mentor and Counsellor. She is very dedicated to uniting cultures under one roof for a great cause & fund initiatives that empower the most vulnerable women and children around the world.

She is a Founder of Ladies of all nations international. Ladies Of All Nations International is a global organization operates worldwide chiefly to bring nations together under the umbrella of humanity with the ultimate goal being to support and uplift the underprivileged in various communities. LOANI is now covering 150 Countries Worldwide promoting Diversity & Inclusiveness covering ALL aspects of Equality &Diversity – including age, race, gender, sexuality, religion, disability etc.

CPSIA information can be obtained
at www.ICGtesting.com
Printed in the USA
LVHW080859110721
692405LV00012B/524